Creating a Criminal

by

E. Frank Bonell

DORRANCE PUBLISHING CO., INC.
PITTSBURGH, PENNSYLVANIA 15222

All Rights Reserved
Copyright © 1998 by E. Frank Bonell
No part of this book may be reproduced or transmitted
in any form or by any means, electronic or mechanical,
including photocopying, recording, or by any information
storage and retrieval system, without permission in
writing from the publisher.

ISBN # 0-8059-4342-0
Printed in the United States of America

First Printing

For information or to order additional books, please write:
Dorrance Publishing Co., Inc.
643 Smithfield Street
Pittsburgh, Pennsylvania 15222
U.S.A.

Dedicated to my wife "Traudel" who suffered alongside Mike throughout this long tribulation of injustice

Preface

Beginning on the next page is a true life story of a typical American family that suddenly finds itself victimized by our criminal justice system. This family's previous experience with and knowledge of the system was limited to high school level education and the influences of our entertainment industry.

The pain, fear, and anguish that were felt by the members of the family is reviewed. The despair they experienced as they slowly learned that each operator in this system had a hidden agenda of personal, financial, or professional gain. The individual that is falsely charged with a crime is not viewed as a human being with rights or feelings but as an object to be exploited by or sacrificed to the system for the benefit of that system.

It was my birthday. Of course, when you reach the age of fifty-four, imminent birthday parties are no longer preceded by that aura of anticipation that had occurred in earlier years.

There was no way that I could have guessed that I would arrive to a house full of chaos! My dear wife was frantic, on the verge of tears. My daughter, Julia, in her normal excitable character, was loudly declaring, "It can't be! Not Mike! It just can't be true!"

I was shocked to learn that my son, Mike, had been arrested sometime earlier that day for having molested his five-year-old stepdaughter.

As my other son, Dave, was arriving with his family, I was rushing out of the door. I mumbled something about having an appointment or such. I don't remember what excuse I concocted, but I had to get to the Tacoma jail office before they closed. I had less than one hour to make bail for Mike.

As I found myself caught in the afternoon commuter traffic, I tried to weave through the stop-and-go gridlock. I was shouting to myself, "That lying bitch! That damned lying slut!" referring to Linda, my daughter-in-law, who had called the police to turn her husband in. My frustration level continued to increase as I attempted to maneuver from one freeway lane into another in an attempt to gain time. I soon realized that each move I made into another lane was costing me the precious distance I was trying to gain. Every lane of moving traffic that I cut into would come to a stop, and I would helplessly watch the vehicles that were behind me in the lane I had just left begin to move past me. Those stoic drivers that just patiently waited as the lanes they were in slowed, stopped, and then started again were getting ahead of me. As I looked ahead down the freeway, I could see a truck about a mile ahead that I had once been behind. As I cursed this unfamiliar evening traffic, my lying daughter-in-law, and just about everything else in general, I decided to take the Port of Tacoma exit. Surely the city arterial would be faster than this stop-and-go freeway traffic. It was not until I was trapped on the exit ramp that I saw the CONSTRUCTION AHEAD signs. "Damn! Damn! Damn!"

It was a lifetime later that I finally arrived at the city-county building. As I noticed the loiterers near the jail entrance, they appeared as if they belonged more inside than outside the place. I had never been to a jail before, and I found that I had to read a series of signs to find my way to the bail office. After waiting in line, I eventually found myself at a screened counter facing a woman wearing a deputy sheriff uniform and whose expression radiated indifference, callousness, and boredom.

"I'm here to bail out Mike Bonnelle," I declared.

After thumbing through a card file, the clerk sounding like a tape recording, said "Do you have a cashier's check for ten thousand dollars?"

"I'll write you a check." I answered, as I unpocketed my checkbook.

"We do not accept personal checks." responded the clerk, in the same, tape-recorded voice.

"It's good. You can call the bank to verify it."

"We don't accept personal checks, only cashier's checks."

"Okay. Okay. Where is the nearest First Bank? I'll get cash."

"We do not accept cash. Only cashier's checks." Looking at her watch, she continued, "The banks are closed now." You could almost hear the click at the end of the tape recorder in her voice.

"Well then how in hell am I supposed to get an innocent person out of your dungeon?" My temper was beginning to get out of control My mind was telling me to control it, but my emotions were screaming that Mike didn't belong there.

"The bail bondsmen are open all night," she volunteered. Her voice was becoming intolerable.

"Which one?" I asked. Suddenly I recalled an episode several years ago when some people had been murdered concerning a bribery situation involving this very sheriff's department and some selected bail bondsmen. It had been headline news for several days at that time.

"We do not make recommendations. There is one across the street, but we don't make recommendations." I expected to hear background static accompanying her practiced responses. I wondered how many years she had been giving the same answers to the same questions. How many years does it take for a person's voice to lose all emotion?

"But doesn't this office close at five o'clock?"

"No. The main jail office closes then, but we are open all the time," she answered. I flashed back to my harried dash to town to meet a now nonexistent deadline.

The bondsman's office looked pretty much the same as any other business establishment. But the look in the bondsman's eyes bothered me. That look reminded me of some pawnbrokers I had encountered many years ago. That greedy look, that "I do anything for a buck" look.

"Ten percent."

"For one night? This will all be straightened out tomorrow. He will only be there this one night."

"It may last longer, weeks, months maybe. You pay us the 10 percent of the bail and we bail him out until it is all over. That is, if you have enough property to cover the entire bail, in case he decides to run." The bondsman haughtily looked me up and down. I suddenly realized what his thoughts must have been, as he, in his nice suit, viewed me in my mechanic's work clothes. Why did I suddenly feel ashamed of my appearance? My dress showed the results of honest work. I suddenly hated the arrogant look on his face.

"He will be released tomorrow. It's all a mistake. One thousand dollars for one night? No way! That's just plain robbery."

"You just might have something to learn." The arrogant face called after me as I departed.

The office of the second bondsman was somewhat less elaborate, but the message was the same. A non-refundable 10 percent of the bail fee. These people were nice enough to let me use their phone, so I telephoned my wife to tell her that Mike would have to remain in jail for that night.

Traffic had cleared by the time I began the twenty-five-mile trip home. Thank God! As soon as I got into my car, I was overwhelmed with fatigue. I was so tired driving home; it had been a grueling three hours.

My son, Dave, and my two daughters, Julia and Tracy, and their children were still waiting to celebrate my birthday when I got home. But it was a joyless celebration which ended early.

I was very happy to see Mike waiting for me when I arrived home from work the following afternoon. What an informative evening was awaiting me. Mike told my wife, Judy, and myself how he had been working on his pickup truck in the driveway of his home when the police arrived. He told us what a shocking surprise it had been to him when they put handcuffs on him and drove him off to jail. Of course, he protested his innocence, but the policemen did not care less. They were busy discussing a recent baseball game. Their job was to arrest people, not concern themselves over whether those people arrested were innocent or guilty of any crime. That was somebody else's problem. They were paid to arrest and jail anybody who had been charged with a crime.

Mike continued, "They took me to jail, searched me, then locked me in a cell. There was nothing in the cell, no table, no chair, no books or magazines, no radio, nothing. Do you know how slowly time goes by when you have nothing to do? By the time they were finished with me, it was past the jail's official supper time. As I hadn't eaten breakfast and was about to get some lunch when I was arrested, I had absolutely nothing to eat yesterday!"

"You're telling us that they didn't allow you to eat anything all day long, and you hadn't even been convicted of a crime?" I asked in surprise.

"That's right, and of course I wasn't singled out. They treat everyone equally, just as if each of us is just some stupid farm animal, unworthy of human dignity. Oh God, I'm so glad to be out of there!"

Judy and I reviewed with Mike his copy of the police report as to what Linda had said to them and the charges made against him.

"This is stupid!" I exclaimed. "She stated that she got up between nine-thirty to ten, which is early for her. What time do the children get up? Who cares for those kids in the morning after you depart for work? You have to be at work by six o'clock. How attentive a mother is she telling us she is? It continues that she watched you molest Sandy for a ten-minute period before she interrupted."

Turning to Judy, I asked her, "Is that what a loving mother would really do? Why, I would think that any mother of a small girl would scream out the moment she discovered the abuse. Wouldn't she hit and kick the molester? Wouldn't she then scoop up her child and run into another room, slamming the door behind her, or maybe run outside and over to a neighbor's house? Would she call the police before or after tearfully spilling the sordid, filthy tale to the neighbor! Isn't that pretty much what would happen at the hands of a loving, distraught mother? The police couldn't see that discrepancy?"

"That's right," my wife answered. "But there is more. I talked to Sandy on the phone at about ten o'clock, and she seemed to be happy and perfectly normal at that time." Then turning toward Mike, she said, "When you called me back, I heard you ask Linda about coming to our house for supper, and everything sounded calm and routine then."

"Yeah, it was," he responded. "But right after that we had an argument. A really big one! Then I went out to work on my truck; I do that when I get really angry. Twenty minutes later, the cops came!"

"Aw, come on!" I said. "I can't believe that Linda thinks anybody is going to believe that she watched you molest Sandy, then let everything return to normal between you two, and three hours later, she suddenly realizes that a crime has been committed against Sandy, so she finally decides to call the cops? No way, no way! Feelings of anger, fear, hatred, and disappointment all subside slowly. I could not just turn those emotions off and then back on again at a more convenient time. "Mike, you don't have anything to worry about. Nobody is going to believe this childish fairy tale."

Then I noticed something that I hadn't seen before. I realized that all during the conversation, Mike had been continuously moving, constantly fidgeting. He would ease himself into a chair, then immediately ease himself up to a standing position.

"What's the matter, Mike? Why are you moving like that?" I questioned.

"Oh, my back is killing me! They took away my medicine in jail."

"What's with your back?"

"Oh, Dad. I've told you before."

"Several times," Judy interjected.

"I have this herniated disk," he continued. "That's why I was home from work yesterday. Actually I've been home for over a week."

"Oh yeah! Now I remember. Say, Mike, let me see you get down onto the floor. Lay on your belly."

"I can't do that, I can't lay on my stomach. It just hurts too much."

I glanced toward Judy to see if she realized the point I was investigating. "I see. Can you get a statement from your doctor stating that you can't lay down on your belly?"

"I don't want to involve him in this!" Mike almost shouted. "This is just too humiliating for me to discuss with anybody. I can't talk about it with anyone but you two, this is just too sick and depraved to talk about."

"Well, I think it's over anyway. If the judge had believed her story, you wouldn't be out of jail now, but you are. The restraining order is for two weeks, you can stay here that long. But you've got to get rid of that bitch."

"That woman," Judy corrected.

"No. That bitch!" I insisted.

"But what am I supposed to do now?" Mike asked. "I can't go home! My cars are there. My clothes are all there. She even has my billfold and my prescriptions."

"Maybe somebody else can go," Judy said. "A third party may be able to get your stuff. There must be somebody that is friendly with you both who could get your belongings from her."

"Yeah, maybe, if she will let me have anything."

Later that evening after Mike had gone to bed, Judy related to me her experience of getting Mike released from jail. She told me that it had started with a court hearing. The judge had reviewed the police report and then released Mike. It was that simple. However, Linda was having a "no contact order" sworn out to prevent Mike from entering his own home. He was ordered not to attempt to speak to Linda, the children, or any member of her family. Judy told me that as she was waiting for the release procedure to finish, much to her surprise, Sandy approached her and said, "Hi, Grandma!" As she held up a stuffed toy animal, she continued, "Look what they gave me at the hospital yesterday." Looking around, Judy then saw Linda and the other children sitting on a bench, apparently waiting for something.

When Linda saw Judy, she turned and asked, "Did you hear what Mike did?"

Judy responded, "I heard the story that you told, but you are going to have to prove it before anybody will believe it."

The next couple of days were pure hell for our family. Mike was trying to get his personal items, changes of clothes, billfold with identification, prescriptions, drivers license, and money. But Linda was reluctant to give him anything. The divorced man living next door had moved in with Linda. The little two-bedroom mobile home soon housed not only Linda, the three children, and the neighbor, but were soon followed by Linda's mother, father, brother, and even a friend of her brother.

Julia, our daughter, was attempting to maintain contact with Linda so as to get messages and requests to Linda from Mike. Julia and Linda had been friends, and if anybody in our family could talk to Linda now, it would be Julia. No other member of the family would be welcome because Linda had correctly perceived that we were maintaining a purposeful distance from her. This had begun when we learned, some time previously, of her affair with Gregg, Mike's brother. However Julia's effectiveness was minimal. Linda was not about to give to Mike anything of value. After much discussion, Julia was finally successful in obtaining some clothing and a billfold that had all the money and everything else of value removed.

One of the items Mike needed was a pack of some insurance forms from his employer, filled in by his doctor, to be returned to his employer to verify his injured back. But that was one of the items Linda refused to allow Mike to have. Therefore, he was forced to return to work or lose his job. It was pure torture for him to attempt to work, but he needed the job. Mike was attempting to get possession of a vehicle. He owned two good cars, a broken-down station wagon, and a pickup truck that was in need of repair. Linda, after a time, did allow Mike's friends to remove the truck and station wagon across the street to Dave Thompson's yard. Mike could work on them there and try to get one running satisfactorily. This turned out to be a mistake. It put Mike directly across the road from his own home, from which he was now denied entry. It also put him within sight of the yard where his children would normally be playing. However, the children were kept inside the home at all times, and all the windows had been covered with heavy blankets. Mike was extremely upset by the vicious acts his wife was doing to him. He deeply loved Linda and wanted a explanation as to why she was hurting him so deeply. He was even more disappointed that the neighbor, whom he disliked, was now sleeping in his bed with his wife. Spending his time in that locality was nearly unbearable. If it did anything positive for him, it was the fact that now the physical pain in his back was less intense than the emotional pain in his heart.

Mike just waited for the no contact order to expire so he could see his children and talk to Linda. During that time, he received a disability compensation check from the state for his back injury, the check was in the amount of $1,000. After Mike cashed it, he put $500 into an envelope and requested that Judy or I deliver it to Linda. Naturally, we refused.

"Mike, why would you want to give her money after what she did to you?" I asked.

"Because she is still my wife and I love her and my children. I want to be sure that she and my children have the things they need."

Judy and I were baffled. Didn't he realize what had happened to him? The vicious woman he purportedly loved had performed the most evil deed possible to him. Yet he was still concerned about her welfare. Was he still in such a state of shock that he did not yet realize that he may need proof of his generous actions and motives? His mother and I finally talked him into getting a money order so that there would be a receipt to prove that he had voluntarily sent Linda the money.

Judy and I had the additional concern of the mobile home. We had purchased it years ago as a rental unit. But we soon found it worked best as a transitional home for our children. As they matured and moved into the mainstream of adulthood, they could begin in their own homes. Although this had worked well for our two other children, this scenario was not working well with Mike and Linda. We had encouraged Mike for several years now to purchase a home of his own. This little two-bedroom unit housing two adults and three children did not work for the well-being of either the family or the home. I recall numerous times when Mike had tried to save some money for a down payment on a home. But each time he got a few dollars set aside, Linda developed a special need that required the savings. The most recent one was a need for braces for her teeth. I thought it odd at the time that a twenty-eight-year-old person who had never experienced dental problems and had no chewing difficulties suddenly required braces. It wasn't unit some months latter when I learned that a woman on one of the soaps that Linda watched daily had required braces. Then her "need" made sense.

Now I realized that my son could not enter my property which I had rented to him. Yet the small home was occupied by four legitimate occupants and five persons who had no business being there.

When the "no contact order" was due to expire, Mike was subpoenaed to attend a court hearing. The hearing was at Linda's request for the purpose of extending the "no contact order." Mike, Judy, Dave Thompson, and I arrived at the court now knowing what to expect. Again, this was a new experience for us all. Mr. Schumacher, Linda's father, and Amber, the youngest child of Mike and Linda, were there with Linda. After listening to the testimony from a couple of married couples and hearing the judge award divorces, it was Mike's turn. The judge listened to Linda's statements, then he read the police report. He then asked Mike if he had been arrested by the police. Mike responded that he had, based on Linda's statements, but he had been released due to there being no evidence. The judge then extended the "no contact order" for a year. Mike was not to talk to Linda or see his children for a whole year. Mike left the courthouse in a state of shock. The judge hadn't even thought about the decision. It was simply a reflexive action. Where was the equal justice under the law!

It was that day or the following day that the harassing phone calls began coming to our home. Our phone would ring, and one of us would answer, "Hello." Then we would hear the click of someone hanging up. This happened five to seven times a day. It didn't bother me. I found it to be humorous. But it was upsetting to Judy. So after a couple days, I tried calling the mobile home to inquire what reason they had for harassing Judy and me. I received a recorded message stating that the number had been changed and the new number was unlisted. As the calls continued and increased in frequency, I advised Judy to not answer the phone. We had a recorded to receive messages when we are not home. We now used it to monitor incoming calls. But Judy stated that she could not put that machine between her and our children, who usually called us every day. I disagreed with her about that. Waiting for a caller to identify himself was not putting a machine between our children and us. They could certainly understand the reasons.

After the extension of the "no contact order," we still had the concerns of a property owner and the fate of our investment in the mobile home. I called several different eviction services and found that their services would not get those people off of my property soon, if at all.

I then drafted a letter using the Washington State Landlord Tenant Act as a reference. I made sure that the letter was within all legal requirements and that it stated the references of my rights as a landlord to inspect my rental property. I gave the time and date of the forthcoming inspection. Then, with my daughter, Julia, accompanying me, I went to deliver the letter. As we drove into the yard, I was overwhelmed at the ugliness of the windows being covered with those dark blankets. Julia stood in the front yard videotaping the event as I went to the front door and knocked. Robert Schumacher opened the door and stood attempting to block my view of the interior. He first looked at me, then glanced past me to see Julia recording our exchange. As he shifted his view back to me, I said, "I have a legal document..." As he reached for the envelope, I continued, "for the legal resident!" As if on cue, Linda appeared behind him, apparently trying to read my lips. As I reached the envelope over Robert Schumacher's shoulder, she reached out and grabbed it. On the way back home, Julia and I laughed as we reviewed how simple the delivery had gone. She really enjoyed how I left Schumacher's hand reaching emptily as I handed the letter to Linda. She was further pleased because sometime during the preceding two weeks, Linda had told Julia not to come around anymore and not to bring anymore messages. Linda had said that there was nothing to be said between our families any longer. That statement had been a consideration of mine in selecting Julia to come with me that day. Therefore, when I returned at the scheduled time and date, to inspect the mobile home, Julia again came as my assistant.

Again Schumacher answered the door. He angrily granted me entry. However, he looked surprised and unhappy at seeing Julia. I'm sure he checked the legal references given in my appointment letter and had consulted an attorney regarding my rights to inspect the residence. But it was obvious that he didn't know what to do about my assistant. As she entered, I said to her loud enough for everyone present to hear, "Your writing is more legible than mine, so you take down all the notes." Linda looked shocked when she saw Julia come in. The situation was now a power struggle as to who controlled the right of entry into the property. The property was legally owned by me. I had complied with the law, and I was not going to flinch first!

As Julia and I began inspecting, Schumacher followed us like a hawk. Within a couple minutes, I sent Julia into another room, but I stayed in the room I was in. As Schumacher couldn't badger both of us, he stuck with me. The conversation began with my finding some damage and shouting to Julia in the next room to write it down. Then Linda appeared from somewhere and said that Mike had caused it. Schumacher added that no damage had been done since he had moved in.

That opened a door for me to respond. So I pointed out to him that our rental agreement called for an additional $100 per month for each additional occupant over the original four. Schumacher replied that they were not residents, only guests. "The law defines guests as persons remaining in a residence for fourteen days or less. You have been here three weeks, which makes you residents. The rent bill for next month will reflect that by including all of you." At that point, he said that they would not be there next month. Continuing the conversation with the intent of gaining as much information about their plans as I could, I learned that they intended to leave on Labor Day weekend. That was five days away, and I was satisfied. Then Schumacher stated, "That was a terrible thing Mike did!"

Looking him straight in the eye, I responded, "A lot of laws have been broken in this matter, but Mike hasn't broken any of them. And if the police thought that he had, he would still be in jail."

"I think he did!" Schumacher countered.

"But the law operates on facts, not on what you think," I said. "If I thought he had done that, I would have called the cops myself. But he wasn't even here at the time. Several laws have been broken, people's rights have been violated, and you can be sure the guilty will pay."

This conversation had occurred as I was inside the master bedroom. Schumacher was in the doorway, and as we spoke, Mrs. Schumacher was in the hallway behind him translating with hand signs to Linda, who was outside my field of vision. The more rapid the conversation, the more rapid her hands moved. I wished I could have seen Linda's face at that time. I had proof that she had fabricated the charges, and she knew it. I didn't know if Mr. Schumacher knew the truth yet or not. I would like to think that he was an honest man who just accepted his daughter's story, out of family loyalty. But I didn't know if this was really the case.

Judy, Mike and I began assembling tools and cleaning supplies to be ready to start preparing the mobile home for sale as soon as those people left, which was to occur sometime the coming weekend.

That Friday afternoon when I arrived home from work, there was chaos in the house again. Mike had been arrested again. The police had gone to his job and arrested him in front of all his co-workers. It required $25,000 bail to get him out or he would be in for the holiday weekend before even having a court hearing.

Judy had already called our stockbroker to inquire about selling some investments immediately to get some money for Mike's bail. They explained it would take about two weeks to complete a sell. But with our investments as collateral, the brokerage house would lend us the money. It would take about twenty minutes for the broker to deliver a check to our door. Judy was still explaining it all to me when the broker arrived with the check. Off we went to the bank to deposit it into our account. We immediately purchased the required cashier's check. Judy was well known at the bank. She was the one who usually made all of our deposits, transfers, and withdrawals. We also have some investments with the bank. Judy and the manager were on a first-name basis. There were only a couple of bank employees who knew me on sight. Even then I was never known as Ed or even Mr. Bonnelle. They referred to me as Judy's husband. The bank teller began to make several phone calls to verify the check from the stockbroker. *Oh, my God!* I thought, a bank should be expected to handle $25,000 checks each and every day. This teller was acting like this was a new experience to her and was treating it as if it were the national treasury or something. I was getting impatient with her slow pace and obvious fear of handling such a sum of money. Suddenly, an assistant manager appeared behind the teller and told her that this was Judy Bonnelle's husband, in a tone of voice that implied that we would get special care. However, even though her speed and attitude improved immediately, she politely explained that she could not see us a cashier's check without her filling in the "Payee" block of the check. Neither Judy nor I knew what the proper title should be. We discussed several options. But knowing that bureaucracies are unrealistically inflexible when it comes to their titles, we went to a public phone. Then came the dilemma of who to call. There was no phone listing for the jail. Should we call the police? There was no non-emergency number listed. Finally I called 911 and asked, "What is the non-emergency number of the Pierce County Sheriff's Office?" Our next call was to ask the phone number of the jail bail office. Then to that office, I inquired, "What title do I put for payee on a cashier's check for a bail payment?"

Judy and I finally got the cashier's check and were off to Tacoma. I insisted that Judy drive this time. However, it was just past peak commuter time. That was the only consolation of being delayed at the bank.

When we arrived at the jail, we went immediately to the bail office and joined the line of people waiting their turns for service. There were people there attempting to get messages or money to their relatives in jail. One young lady was trying to get her car keys from a prisoner's property. Finally we arrived at the front of the line.

"Can I help you?" inquired the familiar inhuman voice.

"Yes. We want to post bail for Mike Bonnelle," said Judy.

After sorting through a card file, the emotionless voice asked, "Do you have a cashier's check for $25,000?"

"Yes," Judy replied, as she pushed the check across the narrow counter.

After studying the check for a moment, the counter woman said, "He will be released downstairs. It'll take about forty-five minutes. You can wait on the first floor."

But we didn't wait. Judy had the name and address of a criminal attorney that she had received from our son, Dave. He had received it from somebody else. This attorney was said to be very good. The office building was easy to find since it was only one block from the city-county building. The entry, waiting room, and receptionist's office were very tastefully decorated.

In response to the receptionist's greeting, we explained that we wanted to discuss our son's situation with Mr. Monte Schuster. We were asked to wait a few minutes. As we sat in the waiting room, I picked up one of the magazines. I was initially pleased that the table was not strewn with last years' *Time* and *Sports World*, as is the case in my doctor's office, my dentist's office, and my insurance agent's office. However, after a moment of thumbing through, I realized that this expensive appearing magazine was actually the advertising medium of some very exotic vacations. These advertised, guided, pampered, and catered trips through the vineyards of Spain were something only the wealthy could afford. Were we in the wrong attorney's office? Was this lawyer out of our class? Judy and I have both come from backgrounds that experienced true hunger. Through experience we had each learned to save not only during good times but also during average times, to carry us through those meager times. The recent years had not been meager. I was now earning well above average wages, and our past savings were now earning some money as investments. Now we were in an attorney's office, not knowing how good he really was, not yet knowing what his fees were, but suspecting he has expensive tastes. Further, we knew of no other criminal attorney, or any way of locating one other than selecting any attorney out of the yellow pages.

The office door opened, and an outstretched hand preceded the smiling face, as a deep, resonate voice said, "Mr. and Mrs. Bonnelle, I am Monte Schuster." A brief introductory handshake was followed by a "Please come in." Within moments Judy and I were comfortably seated, with Monte Schuster on the opposite side of a massive teak desk. We began by telling him how we came to hear of him. He responded by referring to the sources by their first names. Soon we were giving the details of Mike's arrest. We told him of the tensions that developed between our family members and Linda, upon our discovering that she had been sleeping with Mike's brother, Gregg. It had been established that while living with Mike before their marriage, Linda had seduced Gregg, and the resulting affair had continued on after Mike and Linda were married. I had been thoroughly disgusted to learn that Linda and Gregg had been having sex while Mike was taking care of the final arrangements in the church twenty minutes prior to his wedding ceremony to Linda. From the time of that revelation, we lost all trust in Linda. Mike, being unaware of the affair, could not understand why the other members of our family would not accept Linda into our family. But Linda felt the coolness that we felt towards her. It took some time for us to realize that Linda would, on occasion, approach one family member with rumors about that person told by another family member. At first a lot of tension and anger was felt within our family. But after sorting through the stories at a family meeting, it was determined that all of those lies originated with Linda. We told Monte Schuster that we had shielded our feelings from Mike. Mike was blinded by his love for Linda, and he would unconditionally defend her against any negative statements.

Finally Monte said that he would take the case. His retainer was a non-refundable $5,000 up front. He emphasized that expenses could go higher depending on how long and involved things became. He told us that he was very experienced in this type of case, and all the lawyers in the firm were at the disposal of Mike's defense. He explained that he was the Governor of the Board of Directors of the State Bar Association. Judy and I did not understand the significance of that position then, so Mr. Schuster explained that it was a position of status among the lawyers of the state, including prosecutors and judges. Judy and I left the office of Monte Schuster $5,000 poorer but with confidence that we had retained the best attorney possible.

As Judy and I arrived back at the jail, Mike was standing on the sidewalk. It struck me that he seemed to fit in well with the other loiterers, those people whose appearance had disturbed me the first time I had come to the jail. He was wearing dirty, rumpled work clothes because he had been arrested while working. Again I realized that it was not the clothing of the loiterers that was so bothersome, but their facial expressions. Worry, depression, defeat. Yes that was it, the expressions of resignation. Maybe those loiterers were just like Mike, innocent victims that had been beaten down by a blundering, uncaring bureaucratic system.

As we all got into our car for the drive home, Mike was almost in tears. Over and over again Mike thanked us for getting him out of that jail. He had expected to spend the long holiday weekend locked up alone in an empty box. I told him that seemed to be what they had in mind. He continued on that he had no idea that we could come up with $25,000 so rapidly, if at all. We told him that neither had we, but it was now $30,000 and he had a lawyer. Then we spent the rest of the trip home telling him about the lawyer we had hired. We emphasized to him that he had to walk a straight, tight line. If he got in any minor problem, we could loose the bail money.

That weekend was a tense time for us all. We had finally made Mike realize for the first time that this was not a mistake. This was a vicious serious business. Up to this point he had been hoping that an apology would put his life back in order. He slowly came to understand that his marriage could not be salvaged and that he may never see his children again. He accepted the realization that he could actually go to prison for something that he hadn't done. Judy and I were also nervous about the whole situation. We tried counseling, comforting, and advising Mike, but we often ended up arguing between ourselves instead. At night Judy and I would lay side by side in bed, neither one of us sleeping, each lost in our own thoughts. Some feelings, desires, and frustrations are too deep and complex to put into words. We each felt so helpless and so impotent, at the mercy of a system that was too stupid to see obvious lies. As the frustrations each of us felt built up, we released the tension by shouting and arguing with each other.

Saturday morning Dave Thompson called and said that it appeared that Linda and company had moved out of the mobile home. Judy, Mike, and I rushed up there to determine if that was indeed the case. If that was so, we were anxious to put it up for sale. Upon entering the home, the first thing we saw was the emptiness. Every piece of furniture, every towel, every utensil was gone. The only remaining item was a stack of unpaid bills. Some of that furniture had belonged with the home, as part of the rental package, but it all was gone. As we entered the kitchen, our first sight was the kitchen sink. The sink was half full of rotting food. The drain had been forcefully clogged with garbage. We called the Pierce County Sheriff's Department to report the theft of our furniture, then we continued our inspection. We found both of the toilets had been clogged by having disposable diapers jammed tightly down into them. Spoiled food had been dumped down the central heating ducts.

We had expected dirt and wear. We had been aware that Linda was not a good housekeeper. But instead she had just been stupidly destructive. Any house that has been lived in would realistically require some care and repair. But the way the closet doors had been ripped down had to have been done purposely by adults. We were shocked! As we began cleaning up the mess, we questioned ourselves and each other, "What had we ever done to the Schumachers to deserve this?"

Neither my wife nor I had ever raised our voices to Linda or any of her relatives. We had supported the unity of Mike's family at first. During social get-togethers, we had always been polite to Linda's relatives. I liked Robert Schumacher. I had liked his father even more. I detested Linda's mother, Jane, for her domineering manner and insistence that her grandchildren be raised to her specifications. But I never expressed those feelings to her, or to anyone else, except on rare occasions to Mike. Even after our discovery of Linda's sexual experiences, we simply tried to avoid her as much as possible. Of course, with us being aware that she was a pathological liar, I made sure I was never in her company alone. I was afraid of what her incessant lies could do if I was ever in her presence without a witness.

But the answer to our question of what we had done to them, the answer always came out "nothing." But as they had all been present for the destruction of this home, it was now evident that Linda was just another member of a very vicious family.

We were involved with the cleaning and repair of the home when the deputy sheriff arrived. I told him about the theft of our furniture. He seemed to be more than just professionally happy and calm. He was actually jovial as he explained that this was just a misunderstanding among family. He further stated that he was sure that Linda would return our property if we simply asked her for it. He continued, saying that he was a criminal investigator and that this was a civil matter; therefore, he was not allowed to take a report from us. As he joyfully departed I realized that he had spoken Linda's name before I had. As he drove away, I was wondering if he had been another of her many sexual liaisons. My anger was matched by that of Judy's.

"Why?" Judy asked. "Every time Linda calls the cops, they come running and accept at face value any lie that she tells them. But when we call with a legitimate complaint, they refuse to take a report. It seems that if your name is Bonnelle in this county, you don't have any civil rights!"

"That's right," I agreed, remembering that one of the considerations of our having moved our own residence out of Pierce County some five years previously had been because of the sheriff's department. At that time, we had been defrauded out of rent money by a local deputy sheriff. Our efforts to locate him and have him subpoenaed to appear in court after he disappeared from our rental property owing several months rent were undermined by the actions of this same sheriff's department. I had been bitter to learn that the law enforcers were protecting their fellow officer from paying his just debts. But that had been years ago and should have been forgotten by them by now. I guessed that this deputy had been intimate with Linda. I wondered what his feelings would be if he were to know just how many other men she was screwing.

We worked late into the evening, then again on Sunday. Monday was a holiday, so again we spent long hours cleaning. Tuesday was a work day, and I had to return to my job. Judy went to the courthouse to find out what information was available about the charges placed against Mike. Upon her return, she continued to work on the mobile home. I arrived to help after my day at my job. As we were working, Judy told me that she had come across a file at the courthouse with Mike's name on it. It stated that Linda had filed for divorce through an attorney located in the town of Federal Way. His name was Crane. In the statements Linda made in the divorce motion, she claimed that Mike was a heavy drug user. She stated that the neighbor, Dave Thompson, and Gregg were also drug users. She claimed that Dave, Mike's older brother, was growing marijuana in his house. It continued on, each new sentence being more absurd than the preceding one. The filed papers contained one requirement, that being that Mike be subpoenaed at least twenty days preceding the tenth of October, the date of the court appearance on the divorce hearing.

The cleaning, repairing, and painting of the mobile home continued day after day. We were all tired from the long hours. The place began to take on the appearance of a nice, comfortable home. Finally it was time to advertise the home for sale. Judy and I had already decided to ask well below market value, with a large down payment. We wanted to sell it quickly. I was reluctant to leave it vacant for any period of time. The Schumacher family had proven themselves to be so vicious, and we feared they would return. They could also have had friends in the area whom we didn't know. But we did know that vacant homes are sometimes destroyed or torched. Additionally, with all the other problems and frustrations that were accumulating, just disposing of this one would give us some relief.

Surprisingly, we received absolutely no response to the newspaper ad. But a number of inquiries were generated by the small sign I put in the front yard of the home. The property had been on the market for about a week when I got a call from a young man who identified himself as Mike Ranken. He said that he had stopped and looked into the windows and had walked around the place and wanted to buy it. He explained that he did not have all the down payment we were asking, but he expected to receive a work injury compensation check within a couple months. We made an appointment for he and his wife to come to our house the following afternoon to discuss the situation.

That evening, Mike arrived home after having been with his attorney preparing for an arraignment hearing on the criminal charge of child molestation. He had with him a copy of the medical report that was the basis of the molestation charge. The report was on paper headed "Multi-Care" from Mary Bridges Hospital in Tacoma. The report was dated August 29, six days after the alleged molestation. Judy read the report, then handed it to me. Something wasn't right, but what was it? I read the report again. There it was. "Impression: The mother actually witnessed the molestation. Diagnoses: Consistent with Penetration Trauma." "Mike, this is not a medical report. This will never stand up in court. Here, read it over again. Look, this Dr. Dumond writes that she first interviewed Linda. Then she interviewed Sandy, probably with Linda present. Then she performed an examination, after she had already developed the belief that Sandy had been violated. Look at the physical examination. She writes that the measurements of the opening in the hymen is '"4MM in one position and 8.5MM in another position."' Do you know what that means?"

"No," Mike said.

I continued, "Well, I don't know how large 8.5MM is either, but I do know that 7.62MM is 30 caliber, that's three-tenths of an inch in diameter. 12MM is .45 caliber, that's $^{45}/_{100}$ of an inch in diameter. That is absolute proof that Sandy could not have been penetrated in a sexual manner. Why do you suppose that Dr. Dumond writes here that she wants to consult with her colleagues before making a diagnosis? Mike, this whole report is stupid! Have you ever seen a penis smaller in diameter than a pencil?"

"Well, Dad, I'm charged, and that report is the basis of the charges," he said.

"The story Linda gave the doctor here is not even similar to the one she gave to the police, but it is a lot better. I'd bet that what we have here is a doctor who heard a story that had been rehearsed, modified, and practiced for six days to make it believable. And Sandy had to have been coached to tell her tale. The doctor accepted the story even though the physical proof disputed it. So then the doctor asked her co-workers what they thought, and finally, feeling it was her responsibility to serve what she felt was justice, she made a diagnosis based on emotion instead of medical facts. She then wrote, '"The findings are consistent with penetration trauma."'

"Mike, someone is going to read this report while they are studying the police report and the report Linda gave to the prosecutor, then they will see the inconsistencies, and this case will be dropped." I spoke with conviction. "Hell, Mike, if your lawyer puts me on the stand, even I can prove that this is a lie. Back in army interrogation school, we were taught to have a subject repeat their story over and over again. There were several reasons for that, but one important reason was to determine the truthfulness of a story. If the story were true, it would remain the same from one telling to another. Oh, words and phrases would change, more attention to a specific detail may occur, but essentially the story would be the same. But if a person were telling a lie, the story would tend to evolve as the teller himself would detect one discrepancy or another. They would then attempt to improve the story's believability. Look at the evolution occurring between these different documents. The stories here are so dissimilar that they don't even appear to be descriptions of the same incident! This whole affair is just one big lie. It's not even a good lie. Somebody in the prosecutor's office is bound to see this, and the whole thing will be thrown out!"

"But I have charges against me, based on that medical report!" Mike emphasized.

"Yes, you do. But maybe the prosecutor hasn't studied it yet. Actually, Mike, you may have a good case of malpractice against this Dr. Dumond and the Mary Bridge Hospital!

"What about the Good Sam report?" Judy chimed in.

"What Good Sam report?" Mike asked.

"When I picked you up at the jail on the morning of the ninth, Sandy showed me a stuffed bear, and she said that it was given to her at the hospital yesterday. That would have been the day that she was supposed to have been molested. If she was taken to a hospital after you were arrested, she would have gone to Good Samaritan in Puyallup.

"Oh, that must be what the bill is about?" Mike said.

"What bill?" Judy asked.

"Oh, I got a bill in the mail from Good Sam about Sandy going to the emergency room," he replied.

About that time there was a knock on the door. Suddenly the realization flashed across my mind that only a process server would be about at that time of night. I rushed to the door before Mike could get there. I then asked through the closed door "Who is it?"

"Delivery for Mike Bonnelle," a female voice said.

"He isn't here!" I lied.

"But he lives here, doesn't he?"

"No, he doesn't!" I lied again.

I heard departing footsteps, and then we returned to the conversation about the Good Sam report.

"If you weren't charged on the basis of an examination that was made the day of the supposed molestation but were charged on the basis of one made six days later, that first one might be something you would like to look at," Judy suggested.

"Yes, Mike. You need to call the hospital and ask them what the bill is about," I added.

"Oh, they wouldn't discuss a report like that over the phone," Mike countered.

"That's right, they won't discuss the report. But ask about the bill. You don't just pay any bill that arrives in your mail without understanding what it is about, do you?" I questioned.

The following day I arrived home from work to find another chaotic day at home. Judy had received several harassing phone calls. She had been busy trying to catch up on normal household chores which had been left undone while we were preparing the mobile home for sale. Mike had come home from his job barely able to move. His station wagon was running, but it was in lousy shape. He had been assigned to another task at work, one that would be easier on his back, but it didn't eliminate the constant pain. Mike had called the hospital during the day to inquire about the bill. He was shuffled from one person to another, but he finally spoke to someone who could answer his questions. He related to us that he had been told that Sandy had been brought in on the evening of August 8, and she was given a physical examination at the request of the sheriff's department. Thank God! Finally the sheriff's department has done something right. No, Mike could not get a copy of the examination results. That's okay, we knew that the attorney could subpoena the report.

Mike left the house, and Judy and I began discussing the imminent meeting with the Rankens. We ended up in an argument. Judy stomped out of the house. Judy and I have been married more than thirty years, and during that time we had experienced our normal share of differences. But we could always talk about them and come to an understanding. Unfortunately, the stress, anxiety, and fatigue of the last month was taking its toll. We had argued more in the last two weeks than in the preceding two years. We both loved our son, we both knew that he was innocent, and we both wanted to support him in the best way that we could. But we disagreed frequently on what would be effective and what would not.

I was alone at home when Mike Ranken and his wife arrived. They had a small child with them. I was in the embarrassing situation of explaining to them that something important had come up unexpectedly and Judy had to leave.

The three of us discussed their purchase of the mobile home. This was to be their first home purchase. As Judy and I had over the years bought and sold about a dozen houses (thanks to frequent military relocations), we had a lot of information to give them. I explained the pros and cons of home ownership. We discussed different financing styles, taxes, insurance, closing costs, unexpected repairs, and appreciation.

Their situation was that their present rented residence had been sold and they had only two weeks to find another place to live. They had accumulated some savings, but not enough for a down payment and closing costs. Mr. Ranken expected some money from the state within ninety days. We ended the meeting with the understanding that we would have to get together again when Judy was available. I was to phone them the next day. When Judy returned home later that evening, I told her about the meeting. I said that I thought we should agree to sell it to the Rankens.

"What if a problem arises later on, and because they didn't have enough down payment into it, they just let it go?" asked Judy.

"Then we will have to deal with that then. But if that should occur, some of these other problems will have been resolved by then, and we would be better able to deal with that problem. But we are just so overwhelmed with all of these other problems right now, that just delaying this one will give us some relief. Actually, I don't expect any problems. I've met them and you haven't. They kind of remind me of ourselves when we were first getting started. We needed other people's trust and confidence then, too," I encouraged.

That conversation ended with the arrival of Mike. He came in drunk, stating that he had run his station wagon into a ditch. He and I hurriedly got into my pickup truck, which is equipped with a winch, and we headed toward the accident site, some ten mile away. All the way there I was cursing and condemning Mike for drinking and driving. He responded that he knew it was the wrong thing to do, but he was on the verge of going crazy with frustration. I understood his feeling, and he understood my concerns. But the underlying cause of all of our pain was beyond our control. Damn those vicious Schumachers! As we approached the site of the accident, we saw the flashing lights of a police car. As the station wagon was in the ditch on the opposite side of the road, I continued down the road past the site. At the first driveway, I turned around and returned to the scene. I parked the truck in front of the station wagon, setting up to pull it out of the ditch. The patrolman on the scene tried to flag us to continue on, but Mike identified himself as the vehicle owner. After some brief discussion, the patrolman suggested that I look closely at the front end of the station wagon. I didn't have to look close to see that the whole right front wheel assembly was torn loose from the frame. Both the upper and the lower A-frames were hanging free. It would require a wrecker to lift the vehicle up off of the ground and move it. The discussion continued while the patrolman wrote Mike a citation for careless driving. He explained that he could charge Mike with additional charges, but chose not to. A wrecker arrived, then departed with the wrecked station wagon. As we drove home in the truck, Mike said, "This ticket isn't going to do me any good."

I responded, "Just thank God it was the state patrol. If it had have been the Pierce County Keystone Cops, they probably would have shot you on the spot!"

"Yeah, that's probably true!"

The following day when I arrived home from work, I telephoned the Rankens and told them that we would like to sell them the mobile home. They could move in just as soon as they gave us an earnest money check. We then made arrangements to have an escrow company do the necessary paperwork to close the sales contract. I then called the Auburn City police to file a complaint about the continuing harassing telephone calls. Judy had received five calls that day. A police officer came by our home to take a report and explain the procedure to us. We were told that we could take a police report to the telephone company and then have a tracing device put onto our phone line, which could identify the phone number from which each call had come. After that the police could file charges of harassment against the owner of that phone. However, a change had occurred. Prior to the Schumachers having vacated the mobile home, the harassing calls had been coming direct, phone to phone. When we had been working on the mobile home, there had been nobody at our home to answer the phone. But now the calls were coming through operators of a public service named Telecommunication Device for the Deaf (TDD). This aid for the disabled works like this: A deaf person dials the TDD operator, then types their telephone message into a typewriter-like device. The TDD operator then phones the requested number, and after identifying himself, verbally passes the message on to the recipient. Responses from the unimpaired person are then typed back to the deaf caller. With this service, a deaf person can communicate, by phone, with any person he or she desires. Now, a typical day for Judy would consist of six or seven calls with messages like, "This is the Washington TDD operator with....Oh! Your caller just disconnected." Our inquiry to the telephone company resulted in our being told that a tracer put on our line would lead us back to the TDD operator but not through that operator to the actual caller. Therefore, the installation of a tracer would be useless.

When those calls would come, I started telling the operators what was occurring and to not call this number again, as I knew no deaf person who would call me. But the calls continued. Finally I demanded to speak to a supervisor. I was informed by that supervisor that their operators were forbidden by state charter from refusing to place any calls as requested or to request the identify of the caller. I once again stated my position. I was then referred to somebody else in Olympia, the capital city of Washington state. I was once again told of the charter requirements of the TDD service. At that point, realizing that I was now speaking with some bureaucrat, who's stock in trade is reciting documents without addressing the problem at hand, and running out of patience, I flatly stated that I sympathized with the needs of the deaf. However, I had some needs of my own to be addressed! "Wittingly or not, your operators are parties to my harassment. I will not surrender my civil rights to your charter. On receipt of the very next harassing call from TDD, my lawyer will be going to court with the intention of taking away your operating budget, until such time as you rewrite your charter so as to assure that the general public will be protected by it." We received no more calls through the TDD service.

There were only two days left for Mike to be subpoenaed to appear for a divorce court hearing if it were to occur on October 10. We had just eaten a late supper and were now relaxing with mixed drinks. Then there came a knock on the front door. Expecting it to be a process server, I answered the door. I felt confident because I had been recently told that a subpoena had to be given directly to the addressed person or at least placed upon the body of that person. So, when the person on the porch said, "ABC to see Mike Bonnelle," I then turned to Mike and asked confidently, "Did you ever hear of ABC?"

I was shocked when the man threw a sheaf of documents on the porch and hollered, "You have been served, Mike!" The server then darted off into the darkness.

I was really surprised by that action, but I felt sure it was not legal. So I called the local police and reported a prowler being present. When the police arrived, they, of course, found no prowler. But the officer picked up the papers from the porch and said, "It appears like you have been served."

"That's not legal, is it, just to throw some papers on the porch like that?"

"I think so. Good night." And the police were gone.

The next morning I called the number of the attorney who sent the servers, and I asked him what I was supposed to do with those papers. I lied to him, saying that Mike had not been present at the time the papers were left, that he wasn't there now, and that I didn't expect him back soon. But he called my bluff. He said that the server had seen Mike in the house, and he had known who Mike was. What do we do now? Damn, I should not have opened the door!

Mike called Monte Schuster and asked him for a referral to a good divorce lawyer. The governor of the board of the Bar Association should be able to give as qualified a recommendation as anybody. A few days later Mike, Judy, and I found ourselves in the office of one Diane Kelly. We received her sales pitch, which was nowhere near as professional as Schuster's had been. We told her of Mike's situation and came to an agreement. There was something about the woman that made me feel uncomfortable, but I couldn't put a finger on it. Mike emphasized that he wanted to see his children. He hadn't seen them in more than a month, and he missed them desperately. So arrangements for Mike to see them were to be begun by Ms. Kelly. Mike further emphasized that after the divorce he wanted joint custody of the children. But Diane Kelly said, "No. You have to go for full custody or nothing. Going for full custody may be more expensive, but that is the only acceptable route." I wondered, acceptable to whom?

Arrangements were initiated for her to take statements from Mike, myself, Judy, Mike's brothers and sisters, friends, and a neighbor. Also, a statement from Linda's first husband would be helpful, if we could locate him. It was not emphasized, but it was mentioned that all of this statement-taking would cost Mike. It would be $150 an hour. As we departed, we left a check for $2,500 with her.

Within a few days, arrangements were made between the two divorce attorneys for Mike to have visitations with his children. The visits were to be supervised by Mr. Schumacher and myself, jointly. Both grandfathers were required to be present at all times that the visits were in progress. There was also an agreement made between the attorneys and the State Welfare Department. The Welfare people were giving Linda support money, and they were demanding reimbursement from Mike. Mike had up until this time refused to provide money to the state, primarily due to the fact that he had none. The agreement stipulated that the support payments from Mike were to be delayed until after February 28, the date the divorce proceedings were scheduled to go to court.

The visitations were to be arranged and scheduled by the grandfathers. As soon as I was informed of this arrangement, I immediately went to the phone to call Schumacher to get things started. However, I found that the Schumachers had a new, unlisted number. So I waited for him to call me. However, after a week of waiting with no word, I went back to the lawyer. It took two days for Ms. Kelly to get back to me with a phone number. When I called Schumacher, he was surprised that I had his number. But in response to my questions, he indicated that he knew nothing about visitations and would have to check with Crane, the lawyer for Linda's divorce. When a response did not come within two days, Mike and I went to see Diane Kelly. She then called Crane to find out what was going on. She reminded him of their agreement and the court order. Much to everyone's surprise, Crane told Kelly that Mike had threatened Mr. Schumacher earlier that day, and now there was an arrest warrant out for Mike. Mike responded by informing Kelly that at the time the threat was alleged to have occurred, Mike was with his doctor, which would be easy to prove. Then there was a flurry of phone calls between Mike, Ms. Kelly, and a Mr. Percey of Monte Schuster's office to put a stop to any arrest warrant. When the dust settled the following day, it had been determined that there was no police report, there was no arrest warrant, and Mike had a statement from the doctor verifying his location on that day.

Then Kelly presented Mike with a copy of a letter from the district court that said that due to the fact that Mike had threatened Mr. Schumacher and that a letter to the court from a county social worker, named Dan Count, stating that Mike was a child sexual predator, that all visitation rights were now canceled. Mike was devastated! He had already purchased gifts for the children for the upcoming visit. Mike had been anxiously waiting to see the children for the first time in over two months. Mike showed Judy and me the damaging letter. It was typed on Pierce County Health Department stationary. The letter did not use words such as believe, suspect, or think it to be true, but flatly stated with authority that Mike was a danger to children. It continued that all three of his children were afraid of him. The letter was signed by a "Dan Count." But Mike had not been convicted of anything. There were no charges and there was no verifiable truth to these claims.

Then came a letter from Kelly that stated that the $2,500 retainer which we had paid her had been used up. She now required more to continue her services. That was a sad evening in our house. It appeared that Mike had been betrayed by the lawyer he had hired to protect him. His first request to that woman had been to arrange for him to see his children. It now appeared that she had conspired with the opposing attorney to prevent that from happening.

"How much more money is it going to take?" Mike asked.

"Not one damned dime!" I responded. "Look, Mike, what's the point of all of her activity? The criminal trial comes first. If you lose that case, there is no point in all of this. And if you win there, then Linda will be discredited. She will be proven to be not only a liar but an emotional abuser of her children. So the divorce and child custody issues should then be 'cut and dry.' So what's the point in giving this Kelly any more money?"

"But I want to see my kids!" he shouted.

"Yes, I know you do! And I want you to!" I shouted back. "But after Kelly ate up $2,500, what has she done for you?" The prospect of your seeing your kids seems even more remote now than ever before. I'm sorry, Mike, I really am!"

"Why don't you go talk to her, Mike?" Judy asked. "Feel her out, determine if she really believes you. Determine if she wants to help you or if you are just a source of easy money for her? Then you need to do some thinking about whether you want another lawyer." The next day, Mike came home to tell us that Kelly was going to slow down her activities until after the criminal trial was over. She was going to hire a "Guardian Ad Litem" to interview the children and parents. I asked, "What is a Guardian Ad Litem?" Mike told us what Kelly had told him, that the person was an impartial investigator/observer, answerable only to the courts, on the children's best interests.

Then came the charges by a Debbie Lantry. While Mike told Judy and me about what the charges, I sat listening attentively. Some of the sordid tales concerning that neighborhood were known to Judy, but it was all new to me. I was told that the Lantrys lived in the second home to the north of Linda and Mike. Debbie was Linda's best friend, but she hated Mike. The home situated between Debbie's and Mike's was a rental unit occupied by a man named Jim. We were told that Debbie has a fourteen-year-old niece living somewhere in the local area. Sometime in the past year, Jim's wife had returned home to find this niece partially clothed, sitting on Jim's lap, with Jim's hand up the girl's skirt. As a result, Jim's wife had moved out, taking with her their three children. She then filed for divorce. Mike continued, "This niece often visited with the Lantry's ten-year-old daughter. This daughter was experiencing many discipline problems in school, as well as difficulties with other students and teachers. She had been expelled from school several times. Now the Lantry's remained good friends with Jim in spite of what happened to their niece. Linda spoke to Mike about what a nice fellow Jim was. But Jim had cheated Mike out of a couple hundred dollars on some business deal, so naturally Mike had some hard feelings about Jim.

But Linda, among her other failings, lacked the loyalty to her husband that anyone would expect. These stories were coming to me in confused sequences and unrelated bits and pieces, and it required a few retellings for everything to come into focus and proper perspective. WOW! I was overwhelmed! This was more sordid than any soap opera I had ever heard of. However, I needed to understand the background and the people to understand the significance of the police report that had been filed against Mike by the Lantry's ten-year-old girl. That report said that on one occasion, sometime between the beginning of March and the end of June of this year, while passing a baby to the girl, Mike had laid his hand on the girl's breast.

"What breasts?" Judy asked. "She is just a kid, flat as a board!" Mike just looked at Judy and continued reading. The report stated that on another occasion during that same time-frame, while wrestling with several children on the floor, Mike had laid his hand on her underpants. As a result of that police report, Mike was charged with a second count of child molestation. He was scheduled to be arraigned on this charge on the twenty-eighth of November.

"Where was this Debbie when you were doing the wrestling and handing the baby around?" Judy asked.

"Oh, I don't know. I guess she was sitting on the couch talking with Linda," he answered.

"You're telling us that the kid's mother as well as your own wife were in the same room with you when you were supposed to have committed these crimes?" Judy wanted to know.

"And this was supposed to have occurred as early as March and no later than June. Its now the middle of October, and the mother is just now realizing that she saw a crime being committed against her own kid? That's incredible! And the police can't see this scam for what it is? That's even more incredible," I said.

Looking me square in the eyes, Mike said, "Dad, you surprise me sometimes! A deputy sheriff has cheated you out of more than a thousand dollars in rent and theft of property, then the other deputies rally to his side, and you don't get paid. Hell, Dad, you are the one who started referring to them as the Piece County Keystone Cops. How many times have you watched them steal firewood from Weyerhauser land? Now you question their honesty and integrity?"

"No, Mike I'm questioning their intelligence. I always knew they were crooks, but I thought they were smart crooks."

I arrived home from work on the afternoon of November 28 to be told that the arraignment had been rescheduled to December 13. "What really happened?" I asked Mike.

"Nothing. I was supposed to meet my attorney, Wayne Frye, in the hallway of the fifth floor of the courthouse."

"Wait a minute, Mike. Your attorney is Monte Schuster."

"Ah, well," he explained to me, "when you hired Schuster, you were told that all of the attorneys in the office would be available to help me."

"Well, yes, but...." I really didn't understand.

"Schuster was out of town, so now I have Frye. He is an all right guy. But I was to meet him at nine o'clock. He finally showed up at 10:15. He said, 'Hi,' and that he would be right back. He returned at a quarter to twelve and told me the hearing had been rescheduled to December 13." Mike cried, "I just want this nightmare to end! It just goes on and on, getting worse and worse!"

Before the arrival of December 13, my work schedule changed. I was put on second shift, which meant that I didn't have to leave home until about 1:45 in the afternoon. Therefore, it was agreed that I would go with Mike to the courthouse for his arraignment. I had been informed by Judy that she had talked to Frye about getting the bail reduced. Twenty-five thousand dollars was really exorbitant. Frye told her that he would bring the subject up to the judge.

So, on the morning of the thirteenth, I was up at about 7:30, which is early for someone who gets home from work after midnight. Mike and I were off to court together in Judy's car. Again we were to meet Mr. Frye at 9 A.M. in the hallway on the fifth floor of the courthouse. We arrived fifteen minutes early. In the hallway, there was one wooden bench about six feet long and two wooden chairs. So we sat and waited. We waited and watched the people. Lots of people were coming out of the elevators. Most of them had a briefcase with them. Some carried two briefcases with them. There were others who had manila file folders with them. One harried-appearing man, squeezed out of the elevator carrying a stack of five thick folders under his arms. "Five cases?" I silently questioned. "All on one day?" I wondered how much care and attention he could be giving to each of those cases. I began to watch more closely as two men, later joined by a third, were frantically negotiating something at the end of the hallway. There was a man and a woman huddled into a corner comparing documents. The woman pulled a calculator out of her pocket and began slapping the keys. A middle-aged man sat down on the bench beside me. Within moments, he was relating to me that his wife of thirty years was divorcing him. She even had the gall to bring her young lover to court with her today. He continued talking to me until his attorney arrived. Then the two of them began discussing the payment of the remaining $500 owed to the attorney.

My God! I thought, a gentlemen's agreement and a handshake, and the attorney was satisfied. I had paid $5,000 up front, and Mike and I were left here cooling our heels. It was now a quarter to ten. Mike was edgy but quiet. I admired his patience. Patience has never been one of my strong points. I had actually left medical clinics when I wasn't seen within thirty minutes of my appointed time. I would then reschedule for the required services with a competitor's clinic. However, in this courthouse atmosphere, I had no option but to remain and observe the unhappiness around me. I went to the deli and bought a cup of coffee for myself and a soft drink for Mike. When I returned with the drinks, Mike informed me that Frye had arrived and left again. Frye had told Mike that he was attempting to get the matter assigned a courtroom schedule and would be back shortly. Mike explained to me that this was pretty much a duplication of what had occurred on November 28. So Mike and I continued to wait. We waited, and observed the frantically rushing people, the loitering people, and the people huddled into small groups.

This is a public courthouse? I asked myself. This is what we get for all the tax money that we pay into this system? The scenes reminded me of a racetrack where groups of bettors would rush to wager on one horse or another. It also reminded me of huddled soldiers watching the throw of dice over and over again on the heaving deck of a troop transport. Is this what we get for justice in our system? The results of huddled groups of lawyers wagering in the hallway?

I smiled to myself as I contemplated the possibility of this hallway scene being shown in an episode of "Matlock" on TV. Years ago when in high school, I had rushed home after school to watch every episode of "Perry Mason" faithfully. Somehow I had developed an expectation that real life would have the same dignified proceedings portrayed on the TV. But what I was observing now was disgusting. Does the general public know what justice in action really looks like? Finally Mike said to me that I might as well go home. He rationalized that if an available time slot were found for his hearing, it would then be too late for me to attend, as I would have to depart for work before the hearing would be over. I looked at my watch as I left. It was already 11:45. What a waste of three hours.

When I arrived home some twenty minutes later, Judy was waiting. Five minutes after my departure, Mr. Frye had informed Mike that the hearing was again rescheduled. So Judy now had to drive back to Tacoma to bring Mike home. I had to get ready for work. So much for our "torch of justice" on our day in court. The arraignment was rescheduled for December 24, Christmas Eve. As I had the day off work for the holiday season, I again accompanied Mike to court. Mike told me that the same meeting arrangements with Frye had been set up. He told me that Frye had said to him that if they got into court first, it would be over soon. A scene flashed through my mind—a scene of bettors racing to the wagering windows at the local racetrack. The ones who got into the line first got to place their bets, while the slower ones did not. Frye was there on time, and after hurried greetings, he went rushing off to find the prosecutor. Somehow, Mike's name appeared on the next roster posted on a courtroom door. We were ushered into an enclosed observation area. There were large picture windows and locked doors between the observation area and the interior of the courtroom. Mike and I sat down and observed. Inside the courtroom, a person would enter, lay down some papers on a desk, and depart. Then someone else would repeat the performance at a different desk. There was more activity occurring in the observation area. There were several teenagers wearing street gang garb. There was also a large family of Asians loudly speaking among themselves in their own language. There were others also. Some would come, only to depart within minutes. They were replaced by new arrivals.

After a few minutes, the court personnel were assembled and the proceeding began. I found the proceedings to be somewhat entertaining right from the beginning. The first defendant was charged with having stolen something to purchase dope with. The next case was about some woman having pulled out a shotgun against the police during a narcotics raid of her residence. Because she had been wounded by the police, she felt she should be allowed out of jail on bail. We observers were still laughing about that one when a deputy sheriff entered the observation area and called Mike's name. Mike sat looking straight ahead as if he had not heard the deputy. The deputy repeated his name. I nudged Mike to draw his attention to the deputy. He said, "Huh?" Then the officer handed Mike some papers and rapidly left. Mike looked over the papers and then handed me what proved to be a restraining order.

Finally, Mike's turn for a hearing came up. He and Frye were allowed through the locked door. A female deputy prosecutor appeared to press charges against Mike. The deputy prosecutor was absolutely plain in appearance. The most outstanding feature about her was that she wore glasses with pale red frames. It took some time for me to realize that she took effort to avoid eye contact with anyone that opposed her. I found this to be unusual, because eye-to-eye contact tends to emphasize any spoken statement. She was identified as a Sherry Williams. She then read the charges against Mike and asked the judge for a trial date. It was all over in less than five minutes. As we were ushered back into the hallway, I asked Frye, "What about the bail?"

"What about the bail?" he countered.

"I understood that this was to also include a bail hearing. I came to get the bail either reduced or removed. That is why I gave you that list."

When we had met in the hallway at 9 o'clock that morning, I had handed Frye a list to the effect that Mike could not leave the area for the following reasons.

1. Mike has no money or marketable assets.
2. He has no personal transportation.
3. He has no friends outside of this jurisdiction.
4. Every family member, except for one distant aunt, reside in this jurisdiction.
5. Mike is injured and unable to work.
6. Mike is under constant doctor's care and medication.

"Oh!" said Frye. "I didn't know anything about that. This was just an arraignment."

All during the drive home, my mind was reviewing the hearing we had just witnessed. Three different dates and three sixty-mile round trips to court. An excess of ten hours just sitting around and waiting. An equal time for the attorney at a cost of $150 for each hour. There were the numerous telephone calls to the attorney while making the arrangements for the three different occasions. The attorney charges $25 for each telephone call. All of this for just one five-minute hearing that accomplished nothing. I silently wondered, What about those people who have to take time off from work to attend these affairs? What becomes of people without any savings? These people could become indebted to the attorney's for these hearings that become canceled, rescheduled, and delayed. People could become bankrupt then cleared of any wrongdoing by this system of justice. Is this what we were taught in school about our justice system? What happened to "innocent until proven guilty" and "equal justice under the law." Oh my god, I thought, I've been so naive and accepting all of these years. How ashamed I now was for believing the middle school descriptions of our justice system. Little did I know that the disillusionment was only beginning.

We arrived home to sing Christmas carols about peace on earth and good will toward men. I felt precious little good will that Christmas. Instead, I was fantasizing about how best to murder those vicious Schumachers if Mike should go to prison for something he had not done.

Later I talked to Judy about the non-occurring bail hearing. "But he promised me! He said the bail hearing would be part of it," she said.

"Are you sure?" I asked.

"Yes. No doubt about it."

As the discussion continued, it turned to speculation. "Maybe the lawyers just want the money to be available, so if they want more later, they know where it is," I stated.

"I don't know, but we are paying a lot of interest needlessly."

"That may be true. However, I was hoping that when it was pointed out that the basis for such high bail being imposed was based solely on the lies told by Linda, it would be removed. I felt sure that when the prosecutor reread all of Linda's statements, doubt would be raised. It would well be that this Sherry Williams does not yet realize that Linda is a pathological liar. Once she makes that discovery, she may realize that the whole charge is a lie. To just disprove the lies Linda told concerning Mike's capability to leave the area may be all that is required to open Ms. William's eyes.

Judy said, "Maybe we could just talk to her. If we tell her the truth, maybe she would then drop the charges."

"I wish we could, but we have to go through the lawyers to talk to her. It appears that everybody wants this to go to court except us." I spoke with sadness and despair.

"But why?" Judy questioned.

"Money! Money and reputation. The more this is dragged out, the more it costs. I'm beginning to think that nobody but us cares that Mike is really innocent. I'm beginning to suspect that our lawyers just care about how high the bill can be run up. I doubt that we will ever see that bail money again. This is just a game of table-stakes poker. We have ante'd up, and now everybody can see how much more we have on the table to lose. They are just waiting for us to call their raises."

I continued talking, venting my despair, "And that Sherry Williams is just another deputy prosecutor. They are all graded by their superiors on percentages of convictions, of the number of people charged. Their ratings have nothing to do with the actual guilt or innocence of their victims, just the percentages of persons convicted. Hell, the prosecutor doesn't even see Mike as a guilty person, just as an easy conquest."

I continued venting not only my rage at a system that is inherently dishonest but also at myself. How could I have believed all these years that our system would be any fairer or more honest than the systems in Europe and the Asiatic countries I had seen when I was a soldier.

I ranted that our satisfaction would come after Mike was proven to be innocent and charges were placed against those who had concocted this bizarre tale. "And the children, indoctrinating them into telling such lies against Mike must be considered abuse. This has to have been hard on them also. Filing false charges, making untrue sworn statements, it is all against the law. After Mike's case is over, then it will be their turn.

"Mike is fortunate that we have some money saved up to pay the expensive lawyers. None of Mike's antagonists have anything of value. So for their defense, they will have to get court-appointed lawyers. How hard will a lawyer work free-of-charge?"

We finally arranged to have a bail hearing on February 2. I suspected that by now Deputy Prosecutor Williams had come to realize that Linda had been lying. But I really did not know that, I just felt that one cannot know Linda for that long without discovering it. But if she knew that Linda had made it all up, why hadn't the charges been dropped?

At the time of Mike's arrest, the bail had been set exorbitantly high because the judge felt that Mike was a serious flight risk. But the reasoning for that was based solely on Linda's statement. No other testimony had been considered, if heard at all. Linda had told the bail court that I owned an airplane, was a licensed pilot, and that Mike had a sister living in Mexico. There were also other less significant statements.

Now we were ready. Finally, our day in court. We had the documents showing that my pilot's license had been revoked the previous April due to cardiac disease. We had with us the papers concerning the sale of my airplane the previous June, some few weeks after having my license taken from me. With us we had our daughter, Tracy, the one who Linda alleged was living in Mexico. She had with her the rent receipts for her apartment in Auburn for the last three-year period.

As we arrived at the courthouse to attend the bail hearing, we each first went to the restrooms, then we waited for the elevator. As I approached the elevator, Judy whispered, "Schumacher is here! I saw him!"

"Are you sure?" I asked.

"Well, no. But it sure looked like him! He came out of the restroom as you were going in," she added. Suddenly I remembered the little guy that had bolted past me as I had entered the door. He had mumbled hi as he brushed past. I had automatically responded with hello.

When Mike joined Judy and me, I described the hat of the person we had seen and asked him if Schumacher had a hat like it. "Yes, he does," Mike answered.

"Well he might be here!" Judy said.

"What can he say?" I asked. "This is a bail hearing, nothing more."

We met Frye in the usual place, and he said that we could get right in, just as soon as he found the deputy prosecutor. We waited as he rushed off to look for her.

Sometime later he returned to tell us that he could not locate her. We should meet him in the same location at eleven o'clock. We then went to the deli on the eleventh floor for coffee. Just as we entered the doorway, I got a surprise. There sat Robert Schumacher and Mr. and Mrs. Lantry! Seeing them there was quite upsetting to Mike and Judy, so they took their coffee and went to the first floor lobby. However, Tracy and I sat down at the next table with Schumacher's back to us but facing the Lantry's straight on. As I had not known the Lantrys, it was interesting to see what they looked like. I sat there presenting my best air of relaxation and confidence. I was enjoying the discomfort that I was sure I was creating for them. After finishing our coffee, Tracy and I went down to the first floor lobby to join Mike and Judy. We nervously waited in the lobby, trying to guess what those people were doing there for the bail hearing. Mike became so angry, nervous, and frightened that he could hardly speak. So I took him to look for a drug store. I wanted to get him some aspirin or Tylenol. I had learned years before that if taken about thirty minutes before giving a public speech, aspirin would reduce normal tension. I purchased some Tylenol, but Mike refused to take them.

At eleven o'clock, we met Frye in the fifth floor hallway. He had located the prosecutor, and now we had just to wait Mike's turn before the judge.

Finally, Mike was called. Frye addressed the statements concerning the reasons for such high bail and went on to state that it had been based on untrue facts. Then the deputy prosecutor said, "I have no information about that." She then went on to state that the bail was high because Mike had threatened the Lantrys. She called Mrs. Lantry forward, to read a diary of distortions, exaggerations, and outright lies. The judge then asked Frye some questions about the hardships created by the high bail. Frye stammered, made guesses, and basically gave all the wrong answers. We had not discussed with Frye any hardship, so he had no real answers. There had been no rebuttal to the Lantry's lies. The judge decided to allow the bail to ride unchanged.

As we left the courtroom, I felt let down, abused, even raped. My God, what a massacre. With one quick sentence, Williams had changed the subject, presented false testimony, and received a decision from the judge based on only her side.

After some pointless discussion with Frye, we all got into the elevator. There she was. I moved behind and to the side of Sherry Williams, where I could comfortably observe her but where she would have to turn and look up to observe me. She didn't. She stared into the opposite wall above the heads of the other passengers. She would not make eye contact with anybody in the elevator. I studied her intently. In almost every respect of appearance, she was average or slightly below. But her jaw was taunt, and her eyes were steely. She had that look in her eyes that I had seen too many times before. During my twenty years of army service, I had seen that look in the eyes of infantrymen along the Iron Curtain borders. I had seen it in the eyes of American and Korean soldiers alike along the demilitarized border of Korea. And most recently, I had seen it in the eyes of our soldiers in South Vietnam. That hard look of men who have been psyched up for battle. A look that in a kill or be killed situation said, "I am ready to kill all contenders." I stood in that elevator observing Sherry Williams having that identical look in her eyes. I wondered if she had a husband. Probably not. But what if? Oh, that poor bastard! This woman displayed no femininity. She appeared to be devoid of human compassion. The guilt or innocence of her victims would be of no interest to her, only the vulnerability of her prey.

Upon our arrival home, we discussed the court hearing. "God, Mike," I said. "I sure hope Schuster is better than Frye. That was a slaughter. I know that you are innocent, but that wimp can't save you from disaster."

"You're wrong, Dad. He has something up his sleeve. He has a plan. I don't know what it is, but he's got something going."

"Oh, God help us! Mike, that is wishful thinking. If this jerk had anything going for him, he would have used it."

Another sleepless night. I tossed, I turned. I lay there and fantasized all the different ways to torture and murder Linda, Schumacher, and now the Lantrys. I had discovered only two ways to kill one of them with reasonable chance of not getting caught. But each of those two ways could only be used once. Slowly and gradually, the darkness of the night began to fade away from the windows. As the room began to get lighter, the alarm clock went off. Had I slept at all? I didn't think so. As I dragged my weary body from the bed, I hoped I could make it through the new day.

The actual criminal trial was scheduled for February 24. The entire family wanted to get it over with as soon as possible.

Monte Schuster was defending a murder suspect in a trial that was to begin on February 7. I found it interesting that the person being tried for murder was a former neighbor and friend to our sons. Therefore, Mike went to the court proceedings every day to see how the trial was progressing. We all felt that it was important to see how proficient Monte was in court before it was Mike's turn. It still would not be to late to hire a different attorney if Schuster was as bad as I felt Frye was. So each evening we would be told how things had progressed in court. We were told that Monte was an excellent orator that really kept the jury's attention. But we already knew that, what we didn't know was that he had an associate named Brett Percey. Mike would tell us each evening how sharp this Percey was. We were told that Percey would listen intently to the testimony. Then he would whisper something into Monte's ear. Then Monte would do all the talking. But this trial was continuing longer than originally expected. With each passing day, it began to appear that Mike's trial might have to be delayed again. "No, no, no!" Mike insisted. He wanted the trial to occur as scheduled. Schuster was talking about rescheduling for the month of July. "No!" Mike insisted again, "I have not seen my kids since last August. By next July they may not even know me!"

A deputy prosecutor who was present for the rescheduling arrangements said at that time, "But you have visitation rights."

Mike was flabbergasted! "What? Visitation rights? No! Your office put a stop to that."

"I don't think so," this unnamed male deputy prosecutor said.

There was another chaotic evening in our house. As soon as we arrived home, Mike got on the telephone to Diane Kelly. Judy pulled out our file copy of her letters to the prosecutor's office. Kelly got into contact with the "Guardian Ad Litem." As the dust settled, it was determined that the court had awarded Mike visitation rights some months previously, but the prosecutor's office had failed to pass that information onto Mike's attorney.

Arrangements were begun for Mike to see Daniel and Amber under the supervision of the Guardian Ad Litem, a man by the name of Cullins.

Then the trial was rescheduled to take place on March 27. However, Monte Schuster would be unavailable to defend Mike then, so Brett Percey was scheduled to do it. Now we had more disagreement occurring within the family. I wanted Monte Schuster to defend Mike. After all, he was the one we had hired to do the job. He was the one Mike had been most impressed with at the previous trial. He was also the one with the most influence within the legal community. He was that thundering orator whose every word would be grasped at by the members of the jury. But Mike insisted. He just could not continue indefinitely. This torment was eating away at his very humanity. "And after all, it is my life, my family, and my future." He declared. He was correct on each count.

As the days slowly dragged by awaiting the trial date, Mike finally got to visit Daniel and Amber in the office of Mr. Cullins. He came home ecstatic, carrying some still photographs of him and the children. He told us over and over again each detail of the visit. He showed us the pictures of the children, who were happy to see him. Later he said that Cullins suggested that they give prints of the photos to Dan Count so he could see how frightened the children were of their father. It would be nice to present documentary evidence to the judge and jury that Mr. Count's letters were untrue.

Then came the word that there would be a pretrial on March 20. "A pretrial?" I asked Mike. He replied that the prosecution presents its evidence to convince the judge that there is sufficient evidence to have a real trial. They will discuss what is hearsay and what is real evidence. They will determine what will be allowed and what will not be allowed at the real trial. I was getting a real education since this was all new to me. Mike, Judy and I arrived at the courtroom on the tenth floor of the city-county building. This courtroom appeared to be more conventional and attractive than the shabby set-ups we had previously seen on the fifth floor. Mike departed to meet his attorney as we were becoming accustomed to the surroundings. Another person entered. He was wearing clean blue jeans, white sneakers, and a casual shirt. He appeared to be just past college age. Judy and I speculated between ourselves that he must have been one of the policeman who had initially arrested Mike.

As Wayne Frye and Mike entered, Mike introduced him to us, and then the two of them left again to review some notes.

The young man then made a comment that he should have brought a book with him. I responded that I had been thinking the same thing. He then left the room and returned minutes later with a magazine in hand.

Eventually some people began to flow into the courtroom individually. Then the judge entered. The judge seemed impatient and unhappy at the tardiness of the deputy prosecutor Sherry Williams. She arrived some twenty minutes later. After a few brief statements to the judge and recorder, she called Debbie Lantry to give her testimony. Lantry stated that on the afternoon of August 8, she had seen the police cars come to Mike and Linda's place. I really wasn't following her testimony very closely. I knew that she had lied for Linda in court before, so I expected her to lie again. There is not much point in paying close attention to lies. After she ended her testimony, the unidentified man left the room and returned a few minutes later, accompanied by Daniel. The man was then introduced as "Dan Count, Daniel's therapist."

I was angered, so this is Dan Count, the person who had written damaging letters about Mike to the state courts. This person had written letters flatly stating that Mike was a sexual predator, and that his own children are afraid of him. He is the one person most responsible for preventing Mike and his children from seeing each other for more than half a year. During that time, the children had been indoctrinated unhindered. Mike still has not been allowed to see Sandy as a result of this person's lies. As Daniel went by, he looked at Mike, smiled, and said, "Hi, Daddy," to Mike. Daniel, then, still smiling, glanced toward me and Judy. We all looked at Dan Count, as if to inquire, "So is this the child who is so terrified of his father?"

The judge talked to Daniel for a few minutes, satisfying himself that Daniel knew the difference between truth and untruth. Then Sherry Williams began asking Daniel about that morning so long ago. Daniel said he remembered seeing "Daddy on Sandy." As the questioning continued, that same identical phrase was repeated numerous times. However, it was said each time almost mechanically. It appeared that the phrase had no meaning to Daniel but was something that had to be said.

I was watching Dan Count throughout the testimony as much as I was observing Daniel. This Mr. Count sat on the edge of his seat. He was leaning forward with his elbows on his thighs. His fingers were interlocked tightly, causing his knuckles to turn white in color. His jaw muscles protruded with the tightness of his jaw. I realized that although Daniel was relaxed and comfortable, Count was frightened. He was frightened that Daniel would give the wrong answers. For the first time, I began to suspect that Mr. Count was one of those persons that had indoctrinated Daniel and Sandy. Who would be more qualified for the task than a child psychologist?

Up to that point in time, I had assumed that he was just someone who had encountered numerous abused children daily. He had probably just accepted these two kids as additional new members of that unfortunate group, without bothering to give them any kind of a credibility interview. But now he was frightened. Why?

Had he determined, too far into the scenario to turn back, that he had been fooled? If so, he may now be in fear of being held liable for the damage he has caused. Linda was known to have had sex with just about anyone available, so why not him even if he wore a wedding ring. Had she seduced him and now demanded his cooperation in the conspiracy? Who knows? But there has to be a reason for Mr. Count's present terror.

After the prosecutor was finished with Daniel, Wayne Frye asked pretty much the same questions, but in a different manner. The answers were different as to whether Daddy had been dressed or not. Also whether Sandy had been dressed or not came out differently. However, the phrase "Daddy on Sandy" kept being repeated mechanically.

The question kept repeating itself in my mind. Unless this was something of outstanding significance to this four-year-old child, how can he distinguish one particular morning eight months ago unless he had been coached on what to say? The answer kept coming up the same, such an experience would be of no significance to a four-year-old. Therefore, he had to have been told what to say.

Next, Sandy was to testify. The prosecutor stated that Sandy would be coming in accompanied by Dan Count and her grandfather, Mr. Schumacher. "No! No way!" said Frye. "Our agreement was that she was not to be accompanied by any of the family members who she had been closeted with these last eight months!"

"Your Honor, the defense agreed that Sandy would testify!" said Sherry Williams.

"No. Either our agreement is upheld in full or it is off." So she had tried to slip another one in just like she had done with Percey in the bail hearing, but Frye caught it. Good!

I felt so sorry for Sandy. Here she was to look at her daddy and lie about him, encouraged by Dan Count and anyone else the prosecutor could slip into the courtroom. Sandy sat there shaking her head saying, "I don't want to talk about it anymore!"

Next, it was Linda's turn. She got onto the stand, and with an interpreter for the deaf, she told her story. She said that she had woken up that morning and then went back to sleep, then got up again later. She said that she had looked out of the bedroom door and saw Mike molesting Sandy. When she was asked how she could see into the living room from the bedroom door she stated that the bedroom door opened into the living room. But we all knew that there was a hallway between the bedroom and the living room. She continued on with her story, prompted for each statement by the prosecutor. Next it was Frye's turn. During the cross-examination, he asked more specific questions. He requested and received more detailed statements. Then the pretrial was over. The judge and the attorneys discussed jury selection, which was scheduled for the following day.

I had taken a day of vacation to attend this pretrial, but I saw no advantage to witnessing the jury selection, so I returned to work Tuesday. However, after work I rushed directly to the courtroom in Tacoma. The doors to the courtroom were closed, but there was a window in each door. As I looked through a window, I could see that all of the set benches were full. There were some folding chairs that were also occupied. I heard a number being called, and one person get to his feet and moved out of my field of vision. A second number was called, and a chair near the door became vacant. I entered the room as quietly as I could and took the recently vacated chair. As each number was called, a person would get up and move to the jury box. After a period of time, the jury box was filled. The judge thanked those remaining people for their time and then excused them. After the non-selected people filed out of the courtroom, the judge began giving the selected jurors their instructions. All too soon, the day was over. That evening, the entire family discussion was about the jury selection. Mike explained to us how the prosecutor first and then the defense attorneys had asked their questions. Mike felt that he had a good jury. He told us. "They are mostly old folks like you two." I was not encouraged. I know many people my age who may seem wise from experience, but they are really narrow-minded, pig-headed fools, always carrying their prejudices with them. I told Mike this. Judy was as skeptical as I was, but Mike was confident. He stated that one juror had told of having a nephew that had been charged with a molestation and that the charge was all fabrication.

We all slept little that night. Instead of laying awake hour after hour fantasizing how to murder our oppressors in the most gruesome manner possible as I had done so many other nights, I now lay there wondering what baggage the jurors carried with them. I wondered what personal biases they would bring into court with them. It was a long night; the bedroom window grew light very slowly. At work that day, I worried. I counted the hours and minutes until I could return to see the court happenings. But a short time before my work day ended, Judy called to tell me that court had recessed early. I was to return straight home instead of going to the court.

What an evening that became! Our family wanted to have members in the courtroom to give support to Mike and to show the jury that he is a member of a loving family. Judy had planned on being there every day. But Frye said she could not observe the proceedings because that would disqualify her as a witness if it later was decided that she should testify. Julia was next in line, but again, she could be called as a witness, depending on how the tale unfolded. Donna had been the only one present that day in court. She related to the gathered family how Robert and Jane Schumacher sat in the front row and openly snickered and giggled during portions of the testimony. I was never more angry with that whole family. God, how they deserved to die. Neither Mike nor any member of our family had ever done anything to hurt any of them. As I lay sleepless again in bed that night, I was thinking about murder again.

The next day, Wednesday, I left work at 9:00. I was in the courtroom by 10:00. Julia was already there. She told me that earlier that morning it had been decided that she would not testify. Remembering what Donna had told us of the Schumacher's conduct the previous day, I took my place in the center of the front row. Julia sat down beside me. We put on expressions of confidence that we really did not feel.

As the proceedings resumed, we listened to the testimony of a state interviewer from the prosecutor's office who had interviewed Linda on the ninth of August, the day after the date of the alleged abuse. This interviewer presented testimony that was mixed. She appeared to be honest and unbiased. She told how Linda and Sandy had answered her questions, and she presented a typed synopsis of that interview. When it came Frye's turn to cross-examine her, he had her restate that Linda had told her that the molestation had been watched by Linda for a ten-minute period before interrupting. I later learned that a policeman had given the same statement before my arrival that morning. The lady interviewer then continued to answer Mr. Frye's questions. It was discovered that she had to refer to her synopsis frequently. It was also pointed out that after typing the synopsis, she had destroyed the original interview notes. There were some questions that Frye asked which the lady could not answer because she did not have those notes. Frye was really sharp. I began to really feel the confidence that I was displaying as I glanced at Mr. and Mrs. Schumacher, who were now sitting in the row behind Julia and myself. They had very unhappy expressions on their faces today.

After the interviewer's testimony was completed, the judge declared a recess for lunch. It was to be a two-hour recess, as one scheduled witness had not arrived to testify.

As court resumed, Daniel was called to testify. He was escorted into the room by Dan Count. As Daniel took the stand, Dan Count sat on the front row bench at the end. As I looked over at him, I immediately realized that although Julia, I, and the Schumachers were in full view of the jury, Mr. Count was not, since the end of the bench was obscured by the setback of the jury box.

As Daniel's testimony began, I paid less attention to it than I paid to Mr. Count. I had recently studied some interesting books on body language, and now here was a subject that interested me intently. I not only watched him intently, but I found I had to write some notes describing his movements and muscle tones. I was well aware that the Schumachers behind us were watching me watching Count who presented encouraging smiles and nods of satisfaction to Daniel on the witness stand. I watch Daniel repeat his mechanical, obviously rehearsed testimony. God, how I wished the jury could see Dan Count coaching Daniel right here in the courtroom.

The next prosecution witness was Debbie Lantry. She testified that she had seen the police cars parked in the driveway of Mike and Linda's home, so she went over there to see what was going on. Then Linda and the police went over to her house. This testimony was all new to me, and it didn't really fit in with the other stories. But as she was Linda's best friend, the two of them must have cooked up something together. It all seemed irrelevant, since the fact that the police had come and arrested Mike wasn't being contested. Then Frye cross-examined her. But my mind was still on Dan Count. What was the motivation of a professional social worker to lie in court, conspire, and coach children to lie, purposely destroying a person unknown to him, but certainly known by him to be innocent? Why? What weapon did someone hold over his head? After Lantry's testimony, the judge adjourned the proceedings for the day. Court was to resume at 9:00 on Thursday.

Julia and I were seated in the front row again as the jury was brought in. Then the judge entered with the normal formalities. This day, the Schumachers were seated on the third bench from the front. They did not look very pleased. Robert Schumacher looked as if he had not slept a wink; however, ironically, his clothes looked as if they had been slept in for a long time. Were these people finally feeling some of the torment? Was it the same kind of torment that they had so easily heaped upon my family for the last eight months? I hoped so; it made me feel good.

Linda was called to the stand. Sherry Williams began asking Linda to describe the events of the day so long ago. As Linda is deaf, an interpreter was again there to give Linda sign language translations of the questions. Her story was pretty much as expected. A compilation of all her previous statements, but with the most questionable portions of any single statement left out.

I was beginning to really feel wonderful. I knew what evidence Frye had that would prove her story to be untrue. I sat relaxed and smiling. It was obvious that the Schumachers were frightened and unhappy. I watched the jury and tried to determine what their thoughts might be.

There was one woman in the center of the jury box who seemed intentedly involved. Her head would turn toward the prosecutor as each question was asked. Then she watched the interpreter's hand signs. Then this woman would intensely stare at Linda as each answer was given. I hoped she wouldn't develop a sore neck. She seemed to catch even the most subtle parts. Beside her sat a small man with red hair and pale blue eyes. What was he thinking? He appeared to be listening, but he gave no visual indications of his attitudes. Several times during each day of the trial, I would find him staring at me. Why? As I looked into his deep pale eyes, I could detect nothing. Was this juror drunk, drugged, daydreaming? Then there were two old, gray-haired ladies. They looked bored. I tried to determine to what degree, if any, they were paying attention. There were others who just sat there. Suddenly as those pale blue eyes pierced me, I realized that I was the best dressed person in the room. I was wearing a business suit and tie, a stylish shirt, and nice shoes. I looked at Frye's suit, nice but well worn. I looked at the two prosecutors. The man was clean, but his clothes were ordinary. Sherry Williams' dress was of a nice material, but she had a body shaped like a refrigerator with arms and a head attached. The best dress in the world would look like rumpled drapes on her torso.

Of course, the judge wore his black robe. There was no guessing what he wore under it. The members of the jury as well as the Schumachers all looked like they were dressed for a Saturday of household chores. Damn! Was I over-dressed? Would my appearance affect Mike's defense in any way? Should I take off my tie? Would that be a good or bad move? I just didn't know!

Now Frye began to cross-examine Linda. He began by having Linda elaborate on the details of the testimony she had just given. I realized that it was important to have her statement clearly and definitely presented so there could only be one interpretation of what she had said. She again stated that they had received no phone call from Judy, that no calls had been made to Judy, and that Mike had not left the property before the police arrived. These pieces of information were important because Linda had stated that she was too frightened to call the police until about three hours after the molestation because Mike had threatened her life and then he had watched her every move. Frye continued on, asking her about where she had been and what she had done during the day. "Did you go anyplace else?"

"No."

"Did you stop anywhere at all on your way home?"

"No."

As our family was aware of the documented bank deposit slip that Frye had, we could follow his every move as he backed her into a corner of her own making.

Frye then asked her again about how she came out of the bedroom and saw the molestation. He showed her the drawing of the mobile home floor plan, which she herself had made earlier, to verify her story. He then produced a floor plan of the mobile home that had been made the previous day by a professional investigator. This floor plan had been measured and produced to exact scale. Linda became somewhat rattled when Frye showed the two drawings, side by side, to the jury. I had not seen the drawing that Linda had made, but I was later told that she had drawn the bedroom door on the wrong wall of the bedroom. Frye then had Linda mark on the professionally drawn floor plan where the molestation had taken place. The location she identified could not have been seen from the real doorway. Again, the conflicting drawings were presented to the jury.

I looked to the jury. They appeared attentive but unimpressed. I looked at Sherry Williams. Her jaw muscles were bulging with tension. I had felt that for months she had to have known Linda was lying. But had she not known for sure before, she definitely knew it now.

I turned and looked at the Schumachers. They were huddled at the furthest end of the last row of benches. They looked murderously hateful as they muttered between themselves. I had an urge to get up and walk to Schumacher and tell him to check for and eliminate the impossible before he manufactures any more stories for his daughter. But of course I didn't, I simply smiled calmly at him. That drove him into a tightly controlled rage.

Frye allowed Linda to retell portions of her story, considerably changed from what she had said earlier. Now it was time for the defense witnesses. First came Dave Thompson. I had never seen Dave clean before this appearance, but his beard was neatly trimmed and his hair was neatly combed. But most importantly, he didn't appear to be the perpetual drunk that he really is. He calmly related the events of that morning as he knew them to be. He stated that he had gone over with the purpose of telling Mike that he had located a harmonic balancer puller that Mike had wanted to borrow. He continued that Linda and the two children had answered the door. He said that Sandy was wearing pajamas, Daniel was dressed, and Linda was wearing a bathrobe. Linda had told him that Mike was not there, that he had gone to the bank. Dave had then inquired about his children playing with Sandy and Daniel. Linda had replied that she was about to take a shower, but maybe they could play together later. Dave's testimony continued. He said that later he had seen Mike working on his truck and again crossed the street to tell Mike about the puller. Mike replied that he had just bought one. They talked a minute or two, and then Dave had left to allow Mike to continue working, which he did until the police arrived a couple of hours later. The prosecution didn't want to cross-examine him.

Next came Judy. Wayne Frye asked her about that eventful morning, and she related the events as they were now so firmly rooted in my memory. She told of having called Mike and talked to Sandy. She talked about the conversations when Mike called her back. All the details of the background conversation between Mike and Linda were related. Then Frye walked to the defense table, picked up a sheet of paper, returned with it to the witness stand, and presented it to Judy. He asked her if she could identify it. The answer was that it was her telephone bill for the month of August. It was then pointed out that on the eighth of August, a call had been made from our home to Mike's, at about 9:30 A.M. Frye then moved to have the phone record entered as a defense exhibit. When it was presented to Sherry Williams, she displayed contempt at the exhibit but could not give any reason why it should not be entered.

Then Frye said, "I now call Mike Bonnelle to the stand." As Mike slowly rose from his chair and walked to the stand, I thought, *Finally! At last it's finally his turn.* For the past eight months he has suffered insult, humiliation, anguish, despair, torment, and pain. He has had taken from him his home, his family, his every possession, his job, his health, his good name, and for a time even his liberty. No one had cared that he was innocent. No one had even listened to what he wanted to say. How he could have endured this constant torment for eight months was something I could not understand. I don't think I would have been strong enough to live through that. Now as he took the witness chair, I thought that for the first time, he can tell his story. Now the law has to listen to him, instead of blindly accusing him.

As Frye began to question Mike, the story fell together to match what Dave Thompson had told and what Judy had said. But, of course, Mike had been sitting at the defense table throughout the course of the trial. There would be no reason why he could not mesh his story with theirs. As he got to the part about returning home and Sandy telling him about Judy's phone call, Frye again walked to the table. He returned to Mike with a telephone bill from the previous August. It was pointed out that on the eighth, a call had been made from his home to ours. Did the jury remember Linda flatly stating that no calls had come or gone? The juror lady with the swivel head was now leaning forward intently. I thank God for jurors like you, Lady. As the document was presented to the prosecution, Sherry Williams studied it briefly, shrugged her shoulders, and allowed it to become a defense exhibit. Frye continued questioning Mike as to where he had gone that morning. As Frye again walked to the defense table and picked up another piece of paper, I turned to look at Robert Schumacher. He was livid. As Frye handed the document to Mike, it was identified as a bank statement. The document was proof that a deposit had been made that day. The jurors began shifting in their chairs. A tense Sherry Williams, with her male companion, studied that bank paper for a long time. The courtroom was absolutely silent. During that period, which seemed like hours, Sherry Williams studied the document. Was that paper absolute proof that Mike had not even been home at the time that the molestation allegedly occurred? No! There was no time of day for the deposit. But the fact that a deposit had been made and that the phone calls had been documented verified the testimony of the defense. Linda had been proven to be a liar. What would that mean to the jury? Would they believe everything Linda said was untrue?

Finally the day was over. It was Thursday afternoon. The judge declared that Friday would not be a court day. He stated that the lawyers and he would work together on the case, but that the trial would resume on Monday. We understood that since all of the witnesses had testified, the only thing left was the attorney's closing arguments.

That weekend, everyone in the family talked about how they felt better than they had since this all began. I slept better that night than I had in months.

Early Monday morning I had to call my boss and get another day of vacation. Then I dressed in casual jeans, a souvenir sweater from Dawson City, and white sneakers.

As court resumed, we were surprised to hear Sherry Williams recall Linda to the stand. As her questioning began, Williams was asking Linda about the phone calls. Linda answered as if those questions had not been asked before, and answered that the phone calls had occurred. There was no reference to Linda's present testimony conflicting with her testimony of last Thursday. I wished now that there had not been that three-day break. Would all of the jurors remember?

Then Williams asked Linda about the bank deposit. Linda said that Dave Thompson had done it for Mike. In cross-examination, Frye asked Linda if Dave had a ATM card for Mike and her bank account. She stated that Dave borrowed Mike's card all the time. Frye tried to pin her down to any occasion that Mike had allowed Dave to use the card. She had no date when that had ever occurred.

Damn! Damn! Damn! None of the defense witnesses could be recalled, now that they had each sat in the court after having given their testimony. So they were now disqualified. But I was most angry at the damned deputy prosecutor, Sherry Williams. She had now caused Linda to reverse her story. And this public employee, this servant of justice, was now manufacturing evidence to convict a man that she knew to be innocent. Is that what prosecutors see their jobs to be? Only attempts to put people they know to be innocent into prison? Is that what our criminal justice system has deteriorated to? And that woman is as smart and cunning as she is ruthless and vicious. Does she hate men? Maybe she hates everybody. Maybe she is typical of all prosecutors. Maybe they are all lying, criminal scum. I'm just so ashamed of myself for having believed all that propaganda. "Equal justice under the law." "Innocent until proven guilty." "Why would a suspect run if he had done nothing wrong?" It would now appear that those really familiar with our justice system would have become wise enough to run.

I listened bitterly as Sherry Williams presented her closing arguments. Then Wayne Frye presented his closing arguments, pointing out the major flaws in the stories told. I thought that was all, but no. Williams again got up and started to tell the most outrageous lies, innuendos, and personal attacks on Mike. I was happily surprised when the judge cut her off. Even he was repulsed at her conduct. The judge then gave the jury their instructions. The trial was over!

As we were leaving the court building, I asked Frye how Williams had been allowed to lie uncontested. He told me that the prosecutor always gets the last rebuttal. That's the way the system works.

We did not know how long it would take the jury to decide. We waited the rest of the day at the attorney's office, but no call came. Mike had to remain at the attorney's office, two blocks from the courthouse. When the verdict comes in, both the defendant and the defense attorney must be present in court to accept the verdict. However, as Judy and I live some thirty miles away from the court, we could not get back in time to hear the verdict if we waited for it at home.

However, after the court closed for the day, we went home for the evening. I really could not justify in my own mind taking vacation time to await a verdict that may take days. At work, I am constantly on the move, as I have been promoted from mechanic to supervisor. Because I am not normally available in my office to receive telephone messages, I carry a pager. That evening Judy and I devised a list of phony telephone numbers for Judy to call if the verdict came in while I was at work. One number was for guilty as charged, another number for guilty of a lesser charge. A third number was for not guilty, and a fourth number was for a hung jury. And, of course, my real number to have me call home.

The next day (Tuesday), I waited impatiently. At least three times I went to a telephone to call my own pager to verify that it was working. It was, but no call came.

That entire evening, the family discussion was on one subject. What is taking the jury so long? What can they be discussing? Can't they see that no molestation occurred? If only Frye had pointed out....

Another sleepless night. Judy and I lay side by side, each one aware that the other was awake. But what was there to say to each other. We simply each tried to ease off to sleep. Hopeless!

I began another day at work. I was in a staff conference when my pager went off about midday. I looked down at it, and it showed a phoney number. As calmly and inconspicuously as possible, I took out my billfold and removed the piece of paper with the codes. I almost screamed it out! "Not guilty!" I bit my tongue. Nobody at work was aware of this personal family problem. How could anything as controversial and humiliating as child molestation charges be discussed outside the immediate family? It couldn't be, so it wasn't.

As I arrived home that evening Mike and Judy told me of the huge deputy sheriff who had been positioned near Mike as they awaited the verdict. "Just in case I decided to run," said Mike. I thought that it must have been a nice show. But this court on the tenth floor of the building, and the city police department was on the lobby floor. Even if the verdict had been guilty and Mike had attempted to run, there would be no way out of the building without passing the police downstairs. But I had learned by now that the system thrived on powerful displays.

The jurors came down to the first floor lobby as Mike and Judy were there. There were handshakes and thank yous. I was told that the dark-complexioned woman who had been so attentive was the one that had a nephew that had undergone a similar false charge. And that man with the pale blue eyes had asked Judy about me. "What kind of a father could I be?" To be sitting there relaxed, contentedly smiling, appearing to be well entertained, while my son was on trial. That man didn't like what he saw in me. Oh, oh, I had been putting on a false display for the Schumacher's benefit, not for the jury. Those pale blue eyes had sought out and found more dishonesty in this trial than any other set of eyes.

However, Mike had been found not guilty. And that evening there was more joy in our house than there had been in months. As I entered my home, I was greeted with, "It's over, Dad, it's over, and we won. We finally got justice." Mike was so happy as he handed me a Scotch and soda.

"How can it be over, Mike. The Schumachers have not paid for their crimes against you. The county health department that indoctrinated your children to lie against you have not paid for their crime. Even the Mary Bridge Hospital that fabricated evidence against you has not paid for that crime against you. Justice, Mike? They all tried to create a criminal when no crime had been committed. Thank God they failed to accomplish that. But you are still the only person who has lost anything as a result of their efforts. And you have lost everything! Everything, Mike. Everybody except you won, Mike. The police who arrested you justified their jobs by bringing you in. The lawyers would not now have thousands of your dollars if they had just pointed out the stupidity of the first charge brought against you. Most of all, the deputy prosecutor, Sherry Williams. Was she representing the citizens of this county in a search for justice, or was she trying to enhance her own winning percentages by imprisoning a person she knew to be innocent? If your case and all the others like yours had been thrown out, what would that judge do for a living? Your oppressors have lost absolutely nothing, Mike; their every expense was paid for by the taxpayers of this county, state, and country.

When Mike arrived at our front door, we were not surprised at being told he had been subpoenaed once again. The surprise was that this subpoena had come from the Auburn Municipal Court. Ever since Mike had been found not guilty of child sexual abuse of his step-daughter, Amber, in the Pierce County Superior Count, he had constantly been recharged in that jurisdiction on charges of child abuse and/or neglect of one kind or another only to be found not guilty each time. Now Mike and his children were living in Auburn, a short way from us, and Linda was living in Bothel, some thirty miles away. So on her weekend visits, Linda would allow the children to contact head lice, and when Mike would take them to the doctor for treatment, Linda would have a medical record as a basis for a charge of negligence. Linda and her clan had become the joke of the Pierce County District Court. I recall that at the last hearing, Judge Morris had said to Linda that if there were any more of these false charges brought against Mike, he would put Linda in jail. Unfortunately Judge Morris retired one month later; his rulings would still stand but only in that jurisdiction.

So now Linda had turned to the city of Auburn to continue her harassment. It is amazing the amount of harassment a vicious welfare recipient can accomplish through the court systems when it is all paid for by the taxpayers. However, a rational person would expect that a harasser would eventually give up after having never succeeded; but not this group!

When we arrived at the city hall, I expected it to be just another routine hearing. Judy and I were relaxed; Mike had Daniel with him. All that would be necessary would be for Daniel to tell the court about Grandpa Schumacher hitting him, and that would end it!

But as always before, we were confronted with an unexpected complication. The judge said he wanted a Guardian Ad Litem for Daniel, and he then proceeded to appoint Linda as such. We were shocked! Mike went directly to the payphone in the hallway and called his attorney, Diane Kelly, in Tacoma about this extreme violation of Judge Morris's court order. Then all of us potential witnesses had to leave the courtroom.

Although all the Schumacher crowd was huddled together at the other side of the lobby, Dan Count, the Pierce County social worker who was Linda's current lover, wandered away from the group and leisurely started reviewing some brochures on a bulletin board near where Mike was talking on the phone. I had to speak three times before I got Mike's attention and told him to face the other direction and lower his voice, as Dan Count was listening to his conversation.

After Mike got off the phone, he told us Kelly had said not to worry. If Mike won, it didn't matter, but if he lost, then that would be the proper time to raise the issue. I was surprised by her apparent disinterest.

As the jury was being selected, Julia and I found ourselves talking to each other as Dan Count wandered over. As he stuck his hand out to me, he said, "It's important that the truth come out, isn't it?" I took his hand automatically. I shake many hands without thinking about the action many times during the course of my work each day. As soon as our hands touched, I realized I had made a mistake! But the rest of my response was to look at him as sternly as I could with an unwavering steely gaze and said: "I remember how truthful you were during our last encounter!" He returned my gaze just long enough to comprehend my despite and distrust of him. He then turned to Julia, hand thrust out, and said, "I'm Dan Co—"

"I know who you are!" She stated coldly as she ignored his extended hand. As he began to walk away, he again turned to me and said, "All I want is the truth!"

I replied "Your truth is pure falsehood to us! I want justice! Justice for all of us, especially for you!" I held my gaze until he again turned away.

After the jury selection was complete, the trial began with the prosecution witnesses giving their testimony; then there was a recess for lunch.

As our neighbor Bonney emerged from the room, she nervously answered our inquisitive looks with the statement, "I can't talk about the case. I was told that I can't talk about it!" Judy told her we were going home to get some lunch. We then departed. I had to laugh on the way home—actually all the way home. Poor Bonney; she was the neighborhood gossip! She was not just a casual passer of tales, but she was an aggressive, enthusiastic seeker of stories to entertain, enlighten, and frighten her neighbors. Sometimes I thought she could pass out somebody's funeral schedule before the poor soul was even dead. And now she had attended a trial, the first one of her life, and she was prohibited from talking about it!

As we arrived home, I put some soup on the stove, and Judy made some phone calls to check on Amber. Then Mike arrived; he had taken Daniel to school, as the court had decided not to have Daniel testify, so he was allowed to go to school. Mike told us what a stupid bitch he thought the prosecutor was and how the Schumachers kept trying to get hearsay entered in as evidence. He told us how Mike's appointed attorney kept objecting and how the judge kept overruling the attorney.

Then Bonney burst in through the front door, looking over her shoulder to make sure she was not seen. The poor woman must have been in unbearable pain! She could not hold it in any longer! She pretty much verified what Mike had just told us. She had the same opinions of the participants as Mike had just related to us. However, I was happy to have Mike's observations corroborated.

I had always been opposed to bringing Bonney into the family confidence because she was such a gossiper and I realized that whatever family secrets she may have learned from us during a day would be known by the whole neighborhood before the sun went down. This situation with Mike and his children was a private family problem. No one at my job had been made aware of the insults, pain, and anguish our family was suffering. None of our friends and only the closest family members knew. My own parents had not been informed of the despicable lies that had been heaped upon their grandson. We were also concerned about the question of credibility. How can an innocent person prove they are not a child molester?

But Judy pointed out to me that because Bonney and her husband, Jack, were such keen observers, they could testify as to how Mike played with his children in our backyard. They could also testify to dates the children had talked with Bonney, the same dates Linda had sworn the children had not been at our home. After all, Bonney was really harmless; she might be a gossip, but she would never purposely harm anybody. She was a vigorous, but not a viscous, gossiper. Actually I really like Bonney and Jack as neighbors; we get along well, but I would never leave my mail laying around open when she is in my house.

After lunch we returned to court; Mr. Levi, Mike's attorney, quickly asked each of us what testimony we had to give. I told him how Daniel had revealed that Grandpa Schumacher had whipped him and how Dan Count had indoctrinated him into accusing his father of the whipping. Mr. Levi then dashed through the heavy oak doors into the courtroom. "That's it?" asked Gregg, Julia's husband. "Three minutes with Mike's defense attorney, and that's it?"

I responded, "I guess that's it! He is court appointed; he doesn't get paid for this."

Then the testimony of the defense began. First on the stand was Julia. She was followed by Gregg, and then there was a neighbor of theirs named John. That was followed by a recess. Judy, Julia, and Bonney went out to have a smoke. I went out the other side of the building with Mike. He told me right up front he was not allowed to talk about the case! But it didn't take a whole lot of coaxing to get him to open up, and I was a very attentive listener. As we were talking, Dan Count left the building with a very dejected look on his face. "He wasn't allowed to testify," Mike said to me.

"Oh?"

"Mr. Levi pointed out that Judge Morris had declared him to be a prejudiced witness and forbade him from any involvement with the children by court order."

After the recess was over, we all returned to our respective positions—I to a hallway chair outside the courtroom. Suddenly Bonney burst out of the courtroom. She was on the verge of tears, excited as all hell! "He found me in contempt of court! He threw me out for having talked about the case outside of the courtroom! But I didn't! I swear I didn't talk to anybody about his case! I swear it!" I bit my lower lip as our eyes met. She then went charging into the mayor's office. Judy and I were aware she was the recently retired city director of emergency services. She was well known and friendly with all of the city department heads, as well as a personal friend of the mayor. But the Schumachers didn't know that! Having not been in the courtroom but huddled together in the lobby, they remained unaware she had been thrown out. The only thing the Schumacher crowd knew at this time about Bonney was that she was our neighbor. And now they witnessed her burst into the mayor's office and may have also heard a "Hi Bonney" greeting.

As another person entered the mayor's office, we heard a "Well, hi Bonney; how's Jim?"

Now the Schumachers were mumbling together; the deaf ones were almost creating a breeze with their sign language. This really satisfied me. Judy was in the courtroom testifying, so I was alone with my own thoughts. Then Bonney and the mayor walked into the hallway together. As Bonney said her goodbyes, I walked up to the mayor, stuck out my hand, and said, "Hi Bob; it's been a long time." He didn't know me from Adam, but I was counting on his political tact not to embarrass me.

"Yes," he responded, "it has been a long time." As a telephone began ringing in his office, he said, "Excuse me," and disappeared back into his office. I could almost feel a draft from Linda's sign language as I casually returned to my chair.

Now it was my turn to testify. I was prepared. I was going to, at the first opportunity, relate to the jury my story of how Daniel had revealed to me that Dan Count had brainwashed him into falsely accusing his father of the beating.

The swearing in was routine, as was giving my name, address, and relationship to the defendant. Then Mr. Levi asked me if Daniel had told me who had hit him with the stick. I responded, "Yes, he did. It was in our back yard. I had Daniel on my lap and we were—"

"Just answer the question Mr. Bonnelle; we're not here to listen to speeches!" the judge commanded bitterly. For the first time, I looked at him and saw an intolerant, arrogant look on a face that appeared to have had large amounts of booze poured through it.

"Yes, Sir! Daniel told me Mr. Schumacher had hit him with a stick!"

Then the prosecution asked, "When did he tell you this?"

"I don't know when it was!" Thinking rapidly I realized it was during a week day, and it was soon after the charges had been made that I had an opportunity to talk to Daniel.

"You don't know when it was? You have no idea?"

I thought it was supposed to have happened shortly after the weekend of the tenth through twelfth of July. The doctors report was dated the fourteenth. It would have been a few days later. "It must have been about the seventeenth."

"It was on the seventeenth; are you sure?"

"No! I'm not sure; it may have been a day earlier or a day later."

The prosecutor stood up waving some papers. She had the expression on her face of a little girl who had just found a four leaf clover. "Judge, can I show him the dates of these reports?"

Then Mr. Levi asked, "Did Mike get to see his kids the following weekend?"

"No! That's it! He didn't have custody of them yet!" Daniel would not be in our care for another two weeks. "No he didn't; that means Daniel told me about it two or three weeks after the weekend of the twelfth."

"But you don't know when!" The prosecutor was damn near having an orgasm.

"I told you I don't know when it was! It occurred three and a half months ago. I didn't mark it on the calendar. What he told me is extremely important! The time of day or the day of the week are unimportant!" I thundered in response to her.

Again the judge started, "Mr. Bonnelle— " but I wasn't listening to him; I was studying the jury. Most of them looked bored. Not one of them would make eye contact with me. I looked at the prosecutor; she had caught me out of context! But she had not played any masterful plan. She had not devised some brilliant scheme to trick me. I had made the mistake all by myself because I was now used to having the children around our home everyday. Now the prosecutor appeared to me to be stupid. I could not place it as to why; she just looked stupid.

"Mr. Bonnelle, where were you on July twelfth?"

"We were in Pierce County, at Lake Tapps."

"What did the children do there?"

"Oh, they ran around, played in the water, threw balls, rode in a little electric jeep."

"Then you took Daniel home!"

"Me and my wife took Daniel and Amber from Lake Tapps to Puyallup."

"And you turned them over to their mother."

"No. We turned them over to Mr. Schumacher. I think Mrs. Schumacher was there also."

"No more questions your honor."

Back out in the lobby, Judy told me about Bonney's incident. The three women had been discussing who would pick up Daniel after school. Both Judy and Julia were subject to recalls as witnesses, and Bonney was willing to pick up Daniel but didn't know where the school was located. During the discussion, the mayor had come by and greeted Bonney. Then the policewoman who had been in the courtroom saw the three women talking and told the judge. Then the judge found her in contempt for talking, even though his instructions had been "not to talk about the case." Judy was angry about that, and the story she related to me made me angry also. I had already formed the opinion that the judge was an unprofessional, biased egoist. After having been in the state superior court and the country district court several times during the past several months, watching this Court in action reminded me of the TV program "Mayberry RFD" by comparison.

Then an idea hit me: Judy spoke German, and I had at one time been fluent in German but had since forgotten most of it. It had been more than twenty years since I had last been to Europe. So as that policewoman stood by, I turned and said something to Judy in German. Her eyes brightened, and she began relating in German everything that had happened or been said while she was on the witness stand. Of course nobody present understood what she was saying. I only grasped about a third of it. But even that policewoman realized what was occurring as she stood there fuming with anger. Her face got red with hatred as she realized there was nothing she could do about it. It made Judy and I feel very good knowing the policewoman had lost the control of us that was so very important to her.

Finally the time arrived for the jury to file out of the courtroom and into their deliberation room. Mike, as the accused, had to remain at the court to await the jury's decision. The rest of us drove home. As we turned into the driveway, Bonney was rushing across our lawn. Within a few moments of our arrival, Mike telephoned home and asked if Mom would send him something to eat. He was not allowed to have any money to buy anything, and, of course, the courts did not provide food for the defendants.

I arrived back at the court with a lunch for him. Just as the jury filed back into the courtroom: "NOT GUILTY!"

Mike and I arrived home with him still holding his lunch sack unopened. As we got out of the car and approached the porch, Bonney again came charging across the lawn. "It's over," Mike said to her. "I was found not guilty."

As we entered the house, everyone congratulated Mike on winning. But I was confused; he hadn't won anything—he just had not lost his freedom because of another false charge.

But now it is over; Mike is free at last. All of the Pierce County District Court judges now know what liars Linda and her family members are. Although we had cheated as much as possible, they must be sure we have political pull in the city of Auburn. So it is over; no more false charges against Mike will be coming in Auburn. We will now fast-forward from the spring of 1993 and continue at the spring of 1996.

At the end of the school year, it was time for the children to spend two weeks with their mother.

When the day came for the children to be returned to Mike from the visit, Mike found a note on his apartment door asking him to come to the Auburn Police Station. Judy drove Mike down to the police station. When they arrived, they waited in suspense, curious about what calamity had happened to the children. After about twenty minutes, two detectives emerged and arrested Mike on the spot. Judy asked what was going on and a Detective James responded that Amber had revealed to Linda's boyfriend that Mike had molested her. This occurred on a Friday afternoon; the following Wednesday, Mike was taken before a judge in Aukeen District Court. When Mike's turn came, Detective James stood and stated to the judge that Mike had a long history of child abuse charges against him. This was true; however Detective James did not tell the judge that Mike had been tried on each of those charges and the charges were found to be false. Detective james also stated that Mike's family members gave him very negative information about Mike's character. That part of his testimony the detective had fabricated on the spot. As a result of Detective James' false testimony, Mike was put under a bail of $250,000. Knowing this was a family which did not have that amount of money, Detective James smirked broadly as he swaggered out of the courtroom.

Early Monday morning, Judy and I were once again in the office of Monte Schuster. Before we left that office, we had contracted for the services of Mr. Frye again. We could not come up with the required $25,000 non-refundable retainer, but we agreed to make payments. Mr. Frye immediately filed the paperwork to set the court hearing date for twelve days later in King County Superior Court. When the date arrived,

Mr. Frye related to the judge the numerous times Mike had been in court responding to Linda's false charges. Further he made it clear Mike had no history of any criminal conduct, and he had always shown up on time for the court hearings. The judge released Mike on Personal Recognizance. This was a relief to us all, but we all knew this was not the end of the battle. On the long drive home, I asked Mike why he had not called home while he was in jail; he responded that he was not allowed to.

"But I understood that the law says that you are allowed one call," I said.

Mike laughingly said,"Dad, this is Auburn, Washington. They have a phone on the wall, but it has no dial; you pick up the receiver and tell the number you want. But you are only allowed to call an attorney if you know the attorney's phone number by memory. You see, Dad, there are no phone books available. Your billfold and everything else has been taken away from you before you get to that stage of the game."

The next fight would be to have the children returned home. Immediately after having Mike arrested, Linda had gone to work in this well-preplanned conspiracy. She filed for custody based on the fact Mike was in jail and the children would be traumatized at the thought of having to return home. Numerous court appearances later, a judge said this case belonged in family court, not in criminal court.

This was the beginning of a long and depressing episode for this family. We had expected things to continue with the authorities who were somewhat familiar with the personalities involved with this matter. However, that was not to be the case. We soon learned the family courts were overwhelmed with cases and took months for things to occur.

We were introduced to a family practice attorney, a Mr. Dickens. I was pleasantly surprised that his initial retainer was $2,500. I was still stunned by the brief service we had received from our last $35,000 paid to the criminal attorney, but we were saddened by the word it would be months before Mike would see his children again. Those children were Mike's only reason for living, and Linda knew that. Her only reason for wanting the children was to torment Mike and receive state support money. Actually she was living very well on the support money for her six children.

Meanwhile in our household, Mike was getting more depressed with each passing day. When Daniel's birthday came, Mike was almost in tears. Then came Halloween, with all the neighborhood children coming around for treats. That was followed shortly by Christmas, then Amber's birthday.

February finally arrived, and it was time for the court trial of Mike's latest child molestation charge. Judy and I arrived at the King County Superior Court; it had been arranged for us to meet Mr. Frye, Mike's attorney, there. A man approached us and inquired if we were Mr. and

Mrs. Bonnelle, and we responded, "Yes." The man identified himself as Bill Horn; he was sitting in for Mr. Frye, who was tied up with another case in another court this morning.

"But how can you know all, if anything, about this case? It's gone on for years."

"Well this is just an arraignment; all I have to know is the name of the defendant."

So we all just sat silently on the benches as the judge talked. This was all so familiar. Then the court reporter called Mike's name. Mr. Horn, Judy, and I walked forward to stand at a railing in front of the judge. Then a lady, obviously the prosecutor, read the charges against Mike. The judge asked Mr. Horn where Mike was and why he was not present. Mr. Horn told the judge Mike was at work and if he missed another day of work for these court appearances, he would be fired from his job. The judge then asked if Mike had a number of court appearances. Mr. Horn indicated he didn't know. Then I asked, "Your Honor, may I say something?"

"Yes. Identify yourself."

"I am Ed Bonnelle, the father of the defendant. This matter began in August of 1992. Since that time, Mike has been charged five times in Pierce County Superior County before all the judges there learned they were dealing with a pathological liar as a plaintiff. He was then charged in Auburn Municipal Court. He was then charged four times in the Federal Way District Court before the judges there learned that deaf does not mean honest or honorable. So now here we are in your jurisdiction. Mike has not been found guilty of any wrong doing ever!" The judge then turned to Mr. Horn and asked if what I had said was true. Mr. Horn stammered that he didn't know, but he would find out for the judge. I then turned to my right and was surprised to see the woman prosecutor staring intently at me with her mouth agape.

On the way home, Judy said to me, "I hope you didn't cause any trouble."

"Well so do I, but I just had to say something; you know how I am."

The next afternoon, Mr. Frye called and said everything was being put on hold by the prosecutor while they reviewed the charges. The prosecutor also wanted to review the files of all the previous cases. He said he would get back to us just as soon as he had a court date.

Three weeks later, Mr. Frye called and said the charges were being dropped. The prosecutor didn't believe Linda's accusations. We were sure better times were in store for us.

Now it was time to get the children back home where they belong. Judy and I made an appointment with Mr. Dickens and paid him in advance to start the ball rolling. Mike had made it clear from the start that he missed the children and wanted them home just as soon as possible. So we were all surprised when Mr. Dickens told us Mike's case had been put on a back burner for a few days while he took on a case that came in on a later date than Mike's. The whole family was saddened by this betrayal.

Six weeks later, Mr. Dickens was ready to start, but by that time Linda and the children had disappeared and could not be subpoenaed. But we had an ace in the hole and located her ourselves in a matter of days. When we went to give the current address of Linda to Mr. Dickens, he was on vacation. It was in the month of May 1997, before Linda was subpoenaed to appear in court. This time we were to go to the Superior Court in Kent. This was a brand new court; all of the buildings and the parking garage were very nicely built. Judy and I found the correct courtroom, and when we arrived, we met with Mr. Dickens in the hallway. We then entered the courtroom, and we sat down and waited. We listened as several people had their cases heard; this continued on for almost an hour. Finally the Bonnelle case was called; at that time, the court reporter stood up and informed the court that Linda Bonnelle was at that moment giving birth to a child in a Seattle hospital. Later that day we learned that birth was chemically induced, and the scheduling of it had actually taken place the day following her having been subpoenaed to this court hearing. The hearing had to be rescheduled for the first week in July. During the drive home, we had quite a discussion about his surprising development. That birth would have been Linda's seventh child. The first child was from her first husband, who had divorced her. The second and third were from Mike or Mike's brother Gregg. The fourth was from a former neighbor of Mike and Linda, and the fifth and sixth were from unknown fathers. Now this last was probably from her current boyfriend. Also while driving home, we discussed the lack of accomplishment of the day. The only change was that the attorney's fees were adding up; they now approached $5,000. Meanwhile this poor deaf girl—the disabled—received all attorney's services gratis. All filing fees; any costs came to her free of charge. This was great entertainment for Linda and her family. She didn't even have to buy a movie ticket for all of this entertainment. She was the poor little deaf girl who has this sweet young child who has been so viciously molested by her own father, who also unjustly had sole custody of this poor little girl. What attorney would not provide free services for her? Meanwhile the father and former husband are constantly being arrested and jailed for crimes that never occurred. All of his costs must be paid by his parents, who sadly watch tens of thousands of dollars disappear with no justice in sight.

It seemed like it was forever until the next court date, but finally the month of July arrived, and Judy and I found ourselves waiting for Mr. Dickens in the courtroom. On the other side of the room sat Linda with her current boyfriend and three other persons.

In a few minutes, the judge entered and court was in session. Judy and I sat and listened as several persons presented their problems and the judge made rulings, but I really wasn't listening. I was silently questioning

Where the hell is our attorney? After about forty-five minutes into the court session, the court recorder called "Bonnelle versus Bonnelle." I stood and said to the judge that our attorney was not yet present but should arrive at any moment. The judge then called a fifteen minute recess. Needless to say, Judy and I were anxiously awaiting but not knowing if he would arrive. Just as we located a pay telephone and called his office, asking the receptionist where he was, he appeared in the hallway. He explained there had been a detour, and he got lost. As court again opened for business, we listened while the plaintiff presented their case. Then a CPS worker stood up and said the children were safe and happy with their mother and should stay there; blah, blah, blah, and on and on.

Finally the judge, a middle-aged woman, said to Mr. Dickens: "I have read the file you sent to me. I may not have grasped it all—after all it is more than two inches thick—but I have grasped enough to make a decision. Mr. Bonnelle has not been found guilty of anything in the past. But I find it inconceivable that all these charges—from all of these different jurisdictions over a number of years—come with no foundation. So I am ordering Mr. Bonnelle not see or have any contact with his children until he has completed child molester rehabilitation counseling. She then named a counselor in Seattle that was to perform the treatment."

We were all shocked! Later in the hallway, I asked Mr. Dickens why he had not pointed out every one of those charges came from one source, the mother of the children. "Oh, she knows that; you heard her say she understood the file."

"No, Mr. Dickens, that's not what I heard."

"Well we can point it out the next time. This counseling won't take long."

"How long, Mr. Dickens? Mike has not seen his children in over a year."

"Not long, Mr. Bonnelle. I can set it up for you. It will cost about $8,000 for the counseling. Oh, the kitty is just about empty. I'll need another $2,500 to continue with this case. So just as soon as I receive your check for $10,500, I'll jump on it."

"Mr. Dickens, I don't have $10,500."

"You have your house; I can put you in contact with a mortgage company."

"Mr. Dickens, on the seventh of August 1992, I was a happy man; I had a happy family. I had a job that I loved. My wife and I had a home. No, we had two homes. We also had $75,000 that we had saved up for our golden years. Now I am permanently and totally disabled. Constant anguish and stress does that to people. One of our homes is gone; we are now flat broke. My cardiologists are predicting that Judy will be a widow in just a few years. That one remaining house will be her only security. Unless you can guarantee us an end to this constant legal harassment, you're not getting one more cent. In addition to everything else, my son is now a criminal; however, the only crimes committed so far have been against him, not by him. He has been found not guilty in each and every criminal case, but now without a charge being filed against him, without a trial in criminal court, without a chance to defend himself, without the constitutional right to face accusers, he has been decreed to be a criminal by a judge. It was done by a judge that by her own admission didn't understand the history of this case."

"That's not true, Mr. Bonnelle; he just has to get some counseling, and we'll right back on track."

"Mr. Dickens, you know, I know, everybody knows that in that type of counseling, the subject person must admit to and discuss their crimes to a counselor to succesfully complete the course. In this case, Mike would have to untruthfully claim he molested children before he would be allowed to see his own children then be labeled a child molester the rest of his life. Mike wouldn't; he couldn't do that. No, Mr. Dickens, your legal system has created a criminal where no crime has been committed. But you will find that Mike will not participate in this unjust endeavor of your criminal justice system. I have never before been more ashamed of being an American citizen than I am right now."

"Then, Mr. Bonnelle, you're just giving up on the children?"

"No, sir, we are not giving up on the children! We are giving up on you! We are giving up on your court system! We are giving up on your judges! We are giving up on your so appropriately named criminal justice system!"

"What do you mean so appropriately named?"

"I mean it is the most criminal system of justice or injustice you people have been able to devise. But we will still fight for justice for the children anyway we can. You can bet your life on it."

"The court system is the only way," he said. "No member of your family will be allowed to see, speak with, write to, telephone to, or have contact in anyway with your grandchildren until they are eighteen years old. What else can you do: Write a book for them to read?"

"Maybe so, Mr. Dickens, maybe so. But if that is the solution, the book will end with some serious questions—questions for you and for society as a whole."

"What do you mean by that?"

"I mean we have a U.S. Constitution that guarantees us all equal justice under the law. How can there be equal justice when policemen and prosecutors not only can, but are encouraged to, lie in court with impunity? How can there be equal justice when the assets of the state are stacked against the assets of a family? How can there be equal justice when the indiscriminantly accused are jailed while the false accusers are rewarded? How can there be equal justice when every member of your system consider the accused as simply a means of gaining wealth. How can I or you gain equal justice without us all standing up and demanding it?"